Social Issues
in Literature

Colonialism in Joseph Conrad's *Heart of Darkness*

Other Books in the Social Issues in Literature Series:

Social Issues in Literature

Colonialism in Joseph Conrad's *Heart of Darkness*

Claudia Durst Johnson, Book Editor

GREENHAVEN PRESS
A part of Gale, Cengage Learning

GALE
CENGAGE Learning®

Detroit • New York • San Francisco • New Haven, Conn • Waterville, Maine • London

Elizabeth Des Chenes, *Managing Editor*

© 2012 Greenhaven Press, a part of Gale, Cengage Learning

Gale and Greenhaven Press are registered trademarks used herein under license.

For more information, contact:
Greenhaven Press
27500 Drake Rd.
Farmington Hills, MI 48331-3535
Or you can visit our Internet site at gale.cengage.com

For product information and technology assistance, contact us at

Gale Customer Support, 1-800-877-4253
For permission to use material from this text or product, submit all requests online at www.cengage.com/permissions

Further permissions questions can be emailed to permissionrequest@cengage.com

Articles in Greenhaven Press anthologies are often edited for length to meet page requirements. In addition, original titles of these works are changed to clearly present the main thesis and to explicitly indicate the author's opinion. Every effort is made to ensure that Greenhaven Press accurately reflects the original intent of the authors. Every effort has been made to trace the owners of copyrighted material.

Cover image copyright © Lebrecht Music and Arts Photo Library/Alamy.

LIBRARY OF CONGRESS CATALOGING-IN-PUBLICATION DATA

Colonialism in Joseph Conrad's Heart of darkness. / Claudia Durst Johnson, book editor.
    p. cm. -- (Social issues in literature)
    Summary: "Colonialism in Joseph Conrad's Heart of Darkness: Background on Joseph Conrad; Colonialism in Joseph Conrad's Heart of Darkness; Contemporary Perspectives on Colonialism"-- Provided by publisher.
    Includes bibliographical references and index.
    ISBN 978-0-7377-5803-0 -- ISBN 978-0-7377-5804-7 (pbk.)
    1. Conrad, Joseph, 1857-1924. Heart of darkness--Juvenile literature. 2. Colonies in literature--Juvenile literature. 3. Africa--In literature--Juvenile literature. I. Johnson, Claudia Durst, 1938-
    PR6005.O4H47595 2012
    823'.912--dc23
                                                                2011038990

Printed in Mexico
1 2 3 4 5 6 7 16 15 14 13 12

Contents

Chapter 3: Contemporary Perspectives on Colonialism

Introduction

Joseph Conrad's novel *Heart of Darkness*, published in 1899, has often been cited as the most significant work on colonialism in English. It has been a standard text in English literature for decades and has even been the model for a highly regarded twentieth-century film set in Vietnam titled *Apocalypse Now*. To approach the issue of colonialism in Conrad's novel, one must first clarify pertinent terms, specifically, *colonialism, imperialism, postcolonialism,* and *neocolonialism*. The *Stanford Encyclopedia of Philosophy* defines colonialism as "a practice of domination, which involves the subjugation of one people to another." *Webster's Dictionary* defines it as "exploitation by a stronger country of a weaker one; the use of the weaker country's resources to strengthen and enrich the strong one." The word *imperialism* is usually used interchangeably with colonialism, though some scholars make minor distinctions between the two words. Professor Amardeep Singh, for example, writes that colonialism is a practice while imperialism is the idea behind the practice.

The term *postcolonialism*, referring to the period beginning in the mid-twentieth century when colonizers began to withdraw from governing other countries, has been denounced as an unrealistic myth because colonialism has continued to exist in other forms. The word that has more accurately replaced it is *neocolonialism*, in which strong countries and/or multinational corporations continue to exploit the resources of other countries, often with the cooperation of corrupt governments.

Heart of Darkness takes place in the nineteenth century, in one of the more notorious colonial periods, when European countries divided up Africa among themselves. Yet colonialism is as old as human society itself. Marlow, Conrad's protagonist, points this out with his remarks about the Roman invasion of England in AD 43. There were, of course, many colonizers who predated the Roman Empire, including those of the Hittites, the Egyptians, the Macedonians, and the Greeks.

A few of the more notable colonizing events in history include the colonization of the Americas, which began as early as the sixteenth century with the invasion by numerous European countries. In 1612 the English overtook India.

In the nineteenth century, Europeans became fixated on Africa for numerous reasons: abolitionists wanted to find some way to stop the slave trade, missionaries wanted to spread Christianity, explorers were curious about the unknown continent, and, most of all, entrepreneurs wanted to find out what treasures Africa held.

English medical missionary David Livingstone is the first name to come to mind in the exploration of Africa. He was interested in Africa for all the above reasons. For three decades he roamed the continent—from the early 1840s until the early 1870s—becoming something of an iconic figure. Journalist Henry Morton Stanley first gained fame by finding Livingstone in Africa and writing about the meeting. Subsequently, Stanley, from 1874 to 1877, became one of the most recognizable figures working to exploit Africa on behalf of businesses and European royalty. He wrote about his highly publicized voyage down the Congo River to the Atlantic Ocean.

In 1876, King Leopold of Belgium, largely inspired by Stanley's reports of Africa, began his plans to colonize the Congo. In 1878 he set up a consortium of bankers to fund further exploration of financial opportunities in the Congo. From 1879 to 1887, he hired Stanley to represent his interests there. In 1885, Leopold, claiming altruistic motives, made himself head of what he named the Congo Free State. It was not a colony of Belgium; it was his own personal property. His venture there cost millions of lives and bled the country of many resources. The rest of the world, outraged by his blatant greed and atrocities, forced Leopold to relinquish his personal hold on the Congo in 1908. Not until 1960, however, did the Congo gain its independence.

The main action in *Heart of Darkness* takes place in the last decade of the nineteenth century, roughly twenty years after King Leopold declared the Congo to be his private possession. Long after the main action, the protagonist and narrator, Charlie Marlow, relates his experiences to a company of friends drifting down the Thames River. There are two narrators: Marlow and an anonymous one who reports on what Marlow says. Marlow speaks of his success in securing employment on a boat run by a Belgian company that harvests ivory in the Congo. His purpose is to get to the inner station to pick up ivory and rescue, if necessary, the highly successful station manager named Kurtz.

Marlow begins to see the devastation of colonialism even before he leaves Belgium. His experience deepens as he travels through the African forest and reaches the middle station where he observes the incompetence and cruelty of the Europeans who will accompany him on his boat to the inner station. They are attacked by natives along the way (possibly on the orders of Kurtz), but finally reach the inner station, where they find Kurtz dying, his house surrounded by skulls on poles. Kurtz's report on his mission ends with the directive: "Exterminate all the Brutes!" and his last words are "The Horror." Back in England, Marlow lies to Kurtz's fiancée, telling her that his last words were her name.

Heart of Darkness, while it has a secure place in the literary canon as one of the world's masterpieces, is also one of the most controversial works of English literature. There is sharp critical disagreement about what the major focus of the novel is. For many years after the novel's publication, critics regarded it as solely an inner psychological journey, ignoring the social commentary on colonialism. The first three essays in Chapter 2 of this volume counter such an approach, stressing the novel's theme of the plunder of Africa.

A second controversy is over whether Marlow is an ironic narrator. Is Marlow self-deceptive, unlike Conrad himself? Does Marlow see the truth about colonialism? Or does Conrad deliberately present him as a "semi-colonialist"? Finally, there is the spirited discussion, raised by the African novelist Chinua Achebe, who asserts that Conrad's novel is racist and sympathetic with colonialism. Patrick Brantlinger claims that it is impossible to ascertain whether Conrad is a colonialist or an anticolonialist. Frances B. Singh argues that Conrad's demeaning portraits of the colonized Africans undermine any claim that Conrad is anticolonialist.

The articles in Chapter 3 show that colonialism, now called neocolonialism, is still alive and well in the first two decades of the twenty-first century, even though it has taken a somewhat different form. Egregious colonialism involves transnational corporations exploiting developing nations' resources in collaboration with corrupt native governments. These corporations are able to take over vast amounts of the natives' land, displacing farmers, polluting the soil and water—all to make billions of dollars by planting cash crops, drilling for oil, or mining for minerals. So, in the "development" of Africa, for instance, the profits go to the corrupt elite and the multinational corporations outside the weaker countries that they are plundering, while the majority of the native people have no way to make a livelihood, suffer from pollution, and starve for lack of food.

While ivory is the desired resource in *Heart of Darkness*, oil, minerals, crops for biofuels, and cotton are among the most sought after in the neocolonial world.

Chronology

1857
Joseph Conrad is born Jozef Konrad Korzeniowski in Russian-occupied Ukraine of Polish parents.

1862
Conrad and his family are exiled to Siberia.

1873
King Leopold of Belgium begins the colonization of the Congo.

1874
Conrad leaves Poland and trains as a seaman in Marseilles, France.

Henry Morton Stanley begins his three-year exploration of Africa.

1875
Conrad becomes an apprentice sailor in Martinique.

1877
Conrad works on a schooner sailing to the West Indies.

1879
Conrad becomes a seaman on *The Skimmer of the Sea*.

King Leopold sets in motion his plans to colonize the Congo.

1879–1887
Stanley works for Leopold.

1884
Conrad becomes second mate on a ship from Bombay to Dunkirk.

1887–1888

Conrad sails to Singapore, Borneo, and Australia.

1889

Conrad has been fifteen years at sea. He begins writing his first novel in London.

Conrad goes to Brussels to seek a post on a ship to Africa.

Begins journey up the Congo River.

1894

Conrad's sailing career comes to an end and he submits his first novel, *Almayer's Folly*, for publication.

1896

Conrad marries and makes his home in England.

Conrad publishes *Outcast*.

1898

Youth is published.

1899

Heart of Darkness is published.

1900

Lord Jim is published.

1904

Conrad publishes *Nostromo*.

1908

King Leopold is forced to give up his hold on the Congo.

1911

Conrad publishes *Under Western Eyes*.

1924

Conrad refuses a knighthood.

Conrad dies on August 3.

1960

The Congo achieves independence from Belgium.

Social Issues
in Literature

CHAPTER 1

Background on
Joseph Conrad

Conrad's Life as a Sailor and Writer

Monika Brown

Monika Brown, professor of English at the University of North Carolina–Pembroke, has published works on George Eliot's criticism, Gustave Flaubert's Madame Bovary, *and Henry James's* The Turn of the Screw.

Joseph Conrad was born into landed gentry in the Polish Ukraine in 1857. His father was imprisoned for his political views, and he and his family were deported to Russia. After the death of his parents, Conrad was taken in by relatives in Poland. At sixteen he left to be a sailor, sailing from London to places with cultures very unlike his own. He found a job with a company in the African ivory trade and prepared to take a boat to the Congo, where he had always longed to go, and which, at the time, was privately owned by King Leopold of Belgium. The atrocities he found there were said to have killed Conrad the sailor and given birth to Conrad the writer. He went to sea once more after his aborted Congo job, before settling down in England. In 1899 he wrote Heart of Darkness. *Conrad died in 1924.*

The life of Joseph Conrad—a native of the Polish Ukraine who grew up under Russian rule, spoke fluent French, and became a major modern author in English—is as rich and complex as his writing. His fiction and his two autobiographical sketches, *The Mirror of the Sea: Memories and Impressions* (1906) and *A Personal Record*, offer valuable, if not fully reliable, information, and he remains enigmatic in the best biographies, those by Jocelyn Baines, Frederick R. Karl,

Monika Brown, "Joseph Conrad," *Dictionary of Literary Biography, vol. 156, British Short-Fiction Writers, 1880–1914: The Romantic Tradition*, edited by William F. Naufftus, Detroit: Gale Research, 1995, pp. 64–84. Copyright © 1995 Gale, a part of Cengage Learning, Inc. Reproduced by permission. www.cengage.com/permissions.

Zdzislaw Najder, and Jeffrey Meyers. Karl identifies the "three lives" of his subject: an unsettled Polish-Russian childhood, an adventurous young adulthood as a French and British merchant seaman, and a troubled maturity as the British novelist Joseph Conrad, whose subjects derive from his young-adult experience but whose themes are rooted also in his childhood.

Conrad's Troubled Youth

Józef Teodor Konrad Korzeniowski (called Konrad in homage to two heroic characters in patriotic poems by Adam Mickiewicz) was born 3 December 1857 in or near Berdichev, now in Ukraine but then in an area that had been Russian since the late-eighteenth-century partitioning of Poland. The families of both parents, Apollo Korzeniowski and Ewa Bobrowska, were landed gentry devoted to the cause of freeing from its occupiers a Poland that no longer existed as a state. While many Polish nationalists lived in western European exile, Conrad's father, a failed farmer, moved to Warsaw to participate in the plans for the ill-fated Polish insurrection of January 1863. Korzeniowski was imprisoned in 1861 and later deported, along with his wife and their four-year-old son, to Vologda, northeast of Moscow. After the family moved south, to Chernikov, near Kiev, his mother died of tuberculosis in 1865. Four years later his father died of tuberculosis in Kraków and was buried a patriotic hero. Orphaned at eleven, Conrad was taken in by a family friend, then by his grandmother, and in 1873 by his devoted uncle, Tadeusz Bobrowski, whose correspondence with his nephew provides a rich source of biographical information about Conrad.

Though he left Poland at sixteen, Conrad retained an obvious accent, Slavic gestures and dress, and a lifestyle appropriate to a Polish country gentleman. In only one late story, *"Prince Roman"* (1911), did he write overtly about Poland, calling it "that country which demands to be loved as no country has ever been loved . . . with the unextinguishable fire of a hopeless passion." Political issues shape several of Conrad's novels and one story collection, *A Set of Sex* (1908), and the values that pervade his fiction—heroic resistance, grace in defeat, and individualism refined by loyalty to larger causes— reflect a time when, writes Gérard Jean-Aubry, he "unconsciously was trained in a secret and inflexible fidelity to ideals divorced from hope." Conrad's boyhood nurtured modernist attitudes as well, including alienation, rejection of bourgeois values, and pessimism about political reform and the human condition.

Conrad in Non-European Cultures

Conrad received an erratic education from schools and tutors, but literature attracted him. "I don't know what would have become of me," he wrote in *Notes on Life and Letters* (1921), "if I had not been a reading boy." His favorite writers included William Shakespeare, Charles Dickens, Victor Hugo, Miguel de Cervantes, James Fenimore Cooper, and Frederick Marryat. To his readings he traced his impulsive determination, formed at fourteen, to become a seaman, and in October 1874 he left for Marseilles. After training as a sailor and traveling to the West Indies, in 1878 he was ill and in debt. He shot himself in an apparent suicide attempt, which he passed off as a dueling incident.

Unqualified for regular nautical employment without French citizenship, twenty-year-old Konrad Korzeniowski tried his luck in England, which had the world's largest merchant fleet. After early training, including a voyage to Constantinople, in 1879 he began a three-year apprenticeship that took him to Australia and Asia on two clipper ships. During his fifteen years as a British sailor he weathered natural calamities, poor health, a short temper, and poor treatment by superiors. Nonetheless, working hard at his English and at his examinations, he earned the rank of second mate in 1880, first mate in 1884, a master's certificate and British citizenship in 1886, and the command of a small ship in 1888. Lodging in London between voyages, he began a lasting friendship with Adolf Krieger, a partner in a firm of shipping agents who provided loans and other assistance. In 1886 Conrad unsuccessfully submitted his first English story, "*The Black Mate*", to a magazine contest on "My Experiences as a Sailor."

Among the young officer's voyages of the early 1880s to and from southeast Asia, those best known to readers of Conrad's short fiction involve the disintegration and demise by fire of the antiquated ship *Palestine*, which provided the basis for "*Youth*" (1898), and a severe storm and the difficult death of an American seaman suffered on the *Narcissus*. When an 1887 back injury postponed his return to England, he remained in the East. As chief mate on the steamer *Vidar* and as captain of the sailing bark *Otaga*, he transported goods within the East Indies and made excursions to Bangkok, Mauritius, and Australia. As a novelist he would find the Eastern seas his richest resource for fiction. The trying experiences of his first command inspired "*The Secret Sharer*" (1910) and *The Shadow-Line: A Confession* (1917), while stops on Sumatra, Borneo, and other islands brought contact with the character types who would populate his Eastern novels and stories.

The End of His Life as a Sailor

Returning to England in 1889, Conrad expected to receive command of a larger ship, but British sailing ships were reduced by half between 1875 and 1894 as steamships, which were faster and more efficient and required smaller crews, took over international trade. A fascination with central Africa, traced to a childhood curiosity about a blank space on a map, led him to seek work in the Congo (now Zaire) [now, again, Congo], then controlled by King Leopold II of Belgium. A three-year appointment as captain of a steamboat was arranged for him by his friend Krieger and his novelist aunt, Marguerite Poradowska, a resident of Brussels. His experiences in the Congo in 1890, recorded in his first English diary and in letters to his aunt, would inspire his greatest novella, *Heart of Darkness*. After a month-long voyage along the West African coast, he took a small ship to Matadi, the farthest navigable port on the lower Congo River. For the next stage of his journey, a 230-mile overland trek to Léopoldville, his diary recorded hot days, cold nights, mosquitoes, menacing drums, and encounters with corpses and graves. In Léopoldville he encountered a supercilious manager and the news that his ship, the *Florida*, needed extensive repairs. A voyage upriver to Stanley Falls on the decrepit *Roi des Belges* included a crew of African cannibals and the death of a white merchant. Upon his return to Léopoldville, ill with malaria and dysentery, he resigned, his health and nerves permanently impaired.

Conrad the Writer

"It may be said that Africa killed Conrad the sailor and strengthened Conrad the novelist," wrote Jean-Aubry. Between 1890 and 1896 he made the transition to a life of authorship and English domesticity. He worked at sea one more time, now as chief mate J. Conrad of the *Torrens*, a sailing ship carrying passengers to Australia. Its second voyage, in 1893, introduced him to two educated Britons who encouraged his writing: Edward Sanderson, who would succeed his father as headmaster of Elstree preparatory school, and novelist John Galsworthy. In October 1894 Conrad's manuscript of *Almaver's Folly: A Story of an Eatern River* (1895), begun in 1888, was accepted by Unwin upon the recommendation of the renowned editor Edward Garnett, henceforth Conrad's friend and supporter. On 24 March 1896, after the publication of his second novel, *An Outcast of the Islands*, Conrad married Jessie George, a young, pleasant typist with little education. They set off for a six-month stay on the Brittany coast, where he began a novel, *The Rescuer*, and wrote stories for magazines. . . .

The task Conrad set for himself required considerable effort, as he found the act of writing slow, tedious, and frustrating. Conrad based his fictions on facts, his memories supplemented by reading and research. Getting started was difficult, and on an average day, struggling with the English language and his emotional involvement, he produced only around three hundred words. "I had to work like a coal miner in his pit, quarrying all my English sentences out of a dark night," he once told Garnett. When inspiration failed he suffered deep depression. His artistic aims made style important, and he reminded novelist Hugh Clifford in a 9 October 1899 letter that carelessness with language distorts truth, since "things 'as they are' exist in words." Influenced by the Polish language, Conrad's style was heavy with adjectives, parallel constructions, and abstract nouns used for rhetorical effect. The English language challenged but rewarded him: "If I had not known English," he told Hugh Walpole in 1918, "I wouldn't have written a line for print in my life."

By 1899 the forty-one-year-old author of four books and reluctant father of a son, Borys (born January 1898), was settled into his new life. He benefited from literary friendships of mutual respect. The American novelist Henry James responded to a gift of *An Outcast of the Islands* with an invitation, and James recognized the merits of Conrad's best fictions despite finding his pessimism uncongenial. The young American novelist and journalist Stephen Crane asked to meet with Conrad, and the two encouraged each other until Crane's untimely death in 1900. Conrad's friendship was also sought by R.B. Cunninghame Graham, an idealistic Scottish aristocrat, South American traveler, and writer of history books and short stories, who received some of Conrad's philosophical letters. Especially important for Conrad was the support of Ford Madox Hueffer, later known as Ford Madox Ford. From 1898 to 1904 Conrad helped Hueffer become a marketable writer by collaborating on two novels and a novella of slight merit, while Hueffer offered Conrad story ideas, suggestions for his English style, and practical help. In October 1898 Hueffer sublet to the Conrads Pent Farm, near his home at Aldington in Kent, southeast of London, an area where Conrad would live for most of his life.

Between 1899 and 1902 publisher William Blackwood, tolerating delays and demands for cash, serialized in *Blackwood's* and published as books the stories for *Youth: A Narrative, and Two Other Stories* (1902), including *Heart of Darkness* and "The End of the Tether" and the novel *Lord Jim: A Tale* (1900), once intended for the 1902 collection. Among the tales, which narrate adventures of seamen in youth, maturity, and old age, respectively, the first two (like much of *Lord Jim*) are told as reminiscences of Charlie Marlow, Conrad's famous alter ego narrator. *Youth: A Narrative, and Two Other Stories*, dedicated to Jessie Conrad and published in an edition of 3,150 copies, was well received by reviewers and is Conrad's most important collection of short fiction.

Youth: A Narrative modifies the memory/commentary structure of *Karain: A Memory* by presenting the reminiscences of an Englishman capable of reflecting upon his experiences. After an opening in which the frame narrator presents a group of former seamen—"a director of companies, an accountant, a lawyer, Marlow, and myself"—Charlie Marlow, a forty-two-year-old recalling nostalgically but with ironic distance his first voyage to the East at age twenty, begins speaking. . . .

The Subjects of Colonialism and Marlow

Using the same storyteller and structure, Conrad achieved a far darker impact with his masterwork of short fiction. *Heart of Darkness* was written rapidly in February 1899, appeared in three parts in *Blackwood's*, and was immediately recognized as "the high water mark of the author's talent" by Garnett. The frame narrator of "Youth" introduces the same auditors, now on board a Thames cruiser awaiting the tide at dusk, but here he describes both Marlow, who "resembled an idol," and the setting, which reminds him of the great English explorers. Marlow's association is different: "this also has been one of the dark places of the earth." Anticipating the roles that he and Kurtz play in Africa, Marlow imagines two ancient Romans in Britain: the "commander of a trireme" who avoids contact with the wilderness and a young settler experiencing in a savage setting "the fascination of the abomination." Marlow reflects ambiguously on modern imperialism: "The conquest of the earth, which mostly means the taking it away from those who have a different complexion or slightly flatter noses than ourselves, is not a pretty thing. . . . What redeems it is the idea only . . . and an unselfish belief in the idea."

Marlow's account of his Congo journey, adapted from Conrad's experiences in 1890, presents a corrupt system destructive to Europeans and Africans and redeemed by no ideals. Whereas in "Youth" Marlow keeps separate his youthful reactions and mature perceptions, in *Heart of Darkness* he relives his experiences as he speaks, struggling to comprehend them: "to him," explains the frame narrator, "the meaning of an episode was not inside like a kernel but outside, enveloping the tale." The narrative is replete with surrealistic encounters, beginning with the company's shadowy headquarters in Brussels, where two women knit black wool and a doctor studies human skulls and predicts madness. . . .

Critical Controversy over *Heart of Darkness*

Marlow, as a character and a narrator, is also a puzzle. The novella is Marlow's journey: he learns more about himself than about Kurtz. Entranced by the wilderness and by Kurtz, Marlow feels that only his self-restraint and devotion to work protect him from going over the edge. He embodies Western morality and humanity, qualities that Kurtz lost in the jungle. For critic Albert J. Guerard, Marlow's jungle voyage reflects

Joseph Conrad in 1923. © Hulton Archive/Getty Images.

the archetypal hero's journey to self-discovery in a dreamlike world where he confronts his suppressed double, or "shadow." Karl, who identifies Kurtz with the id and the desire in individuals and civilizations for unrestrained power, sees in Marlow the rational side of human nature that confronts and restrains these impulses. Critics have puzzled over Marlow's decision, in a portentous final scene in Brussels, to lie to Kurtz's pale and elegant "Intended" by telling her, because the truth is "too dark altogether," that Kurtz's last words were "your name." For feminists Marlow's lie shows condescension, while Karl believes that the lie helps Marlow preserve his own illusions about Kurtz. Others see Marlow's lie as a humane act that distances him from Kurtz's merciless absolutes of good and evil.

Critical understanding of Marlow is bound up also with responses to Conrad's style, imagery, and atmosphere in *Heart of Darkness*. The *Manchester Guardian* reviewer was impressed by Conrad's style, but poet and novelist John Masefield noted that the "stately and brilliant prose . . . gives one a curious impression of remoteness and aloofness from its subject." F.R. Leavis admires Conrad's precise descriptions and "sinister and fantastic 'atmosphere'" but criticizes as morally irresponsible his vague philosophizing about the unspeakable. Other critics consider his verbal ambiguities appropriate to a dream journey.

Conrad's stands on social, racial, and gender issues were debated from the start. The *Manchester Guardian* noted that while the novella does not directly attack imperialism, "cheap ideals, platitudes of civilization are shrivelled up in the heat of such experiences." More recently, Nigerian novelist Chinua Achebe—author of an alternative fictional portrayal of colonization, *Things Fall Apart* (1958)—has concluded that Conrad "was a thoroughgoing racist" who uses "Africa as setting and backdrop which eliminates the African as human factor." West Indian novelist V.S. Naipaul explicitly adapted motifs from *Heart of Darkness* for *A Bend in the River* (1979), set in postcolonial Zaire, and filmmaker Francis Ford Coppola, in *Apocalypse Now* (1979), drew from Conrad's novella symbols that indict a modern evil, America's involvement in Vietnam and Cambodia. . . .

Conrad's Last Decade

The last decade of Conrad's life was his most successful professionally, and he recognized the irony of his celebrity status, which allowed his later works to appear in large editions and earn far more money than his best writings. He issued a collected American edition of his works in 1921 and a deluxe British edition in 1922; sold manuscripts and film rights; wrote a silent-film scenario, "The Strong Man," based on "Gaspar Ruiz," and a play based on *The Secret Agent* (1921); and settled in 1919 in a stately old residence, Oswalds, in Bishopsbourne, near Canterbury. In 1920 he made a new friend, the adventurer T.E. Lawrence, and in 1922 suffered the death of his close friend and agent [James] Pinker.

The American publisher Frank Doubleday persuaded Conrad to travel across the Atlantic in 1923. Highlights of this stressful trip included travel through New England and a lecture in New York City to a select audience, whom he moved to tears by reading from *Victory*. He declined a knighthood in 1924 along with offers of honorary degrees from several British universities; he never received the one award he coveted, the Nobel Prize. On 3 August 1924, at age sixty-six, Conrad died of a heart attack. A Catholic funeral was arranged on 7 August at St. Thomas's Catholic Church, Canterbury, by his wife, who was too crippled to attend. On the granite tombstone was carved a quotation from Edmund Spenser's *The Faerie Queene* (1590, 1596): "Sleep after toyle, port after stormie seas, / Ease after warre, death after life does greatly please."

The Destruction of Conrad's Colonial Ideal

Jeffrey Meyers

Jeffrey Meyers is a prolific and distinguished biographer and an emeritus professor. He is one of only a dozen Americans who are fellows in the British Royal Society of Literature.

Joseph Conrad had to struggle as a young sailor for jobs aboard ships, and when he did go to sea, the experience was invariably unpleasant. His first assignments were to Asia, but his compelling urge was to go to Africa. His colonial ideal was destroyed by his introduction to reality in the Congo, largely through reformer Roger Casement with whom he shared a room there. Casement, a hunter and explorer and later a consul, took Conrad with him on his visits to various tribes. By the time Conrad returned from the Congo, he was suffering from physical and psychological ailments that would haunt him for the rest of his life. Casement's 1903 report on colonialism, contending that the colonizers were more savage than the natives and detailing the atrocities in the Congo, not only forced King Leopold to relinquish his personal hold on the Congo but also greatly influenced the writing of Heart of Darkness.

During the seventeen long months on land between leaving the *Otago* in Adelaide and boarding the *Roi des Belges* in Kinshasa (March 1889–August 1890), Conrad had ample time to reflect on the unsuccessful course of his maritime service. The "Polish nobleman, cased in British tar" [as he onced described himself] had, by extraordinary effort, worked his way up from ordinary seaman to captain. But his career was stagnant and he found it extremely hard to get a job. It was

Jeffrey Meyers, "Into the Congo, 1890," in *Joseph Conrad: A Biography*, New York: Charles Scribner's Sons, 1991, pp. 91–92, 95–97, 99–102, 107–108. Reproduced by permission.

difficult to have the right connections and the right luck, to be on the scene when the appropriate ship was available, to have the necessary qualifications and to make the right impression.

The struggle to find a berth was often followed by bad experiences on board. The *Tremolino* had been wrecked near Marseilles; he had been excluded, for political reasons, from service on French ships; had quarreled with the master of the *Mavis* and lost his deposit; had been exploited by the mad captain of the *Europa*. He had not completed the round-trip voyages on the *Palestine* or on the *Riversdale*. He had a series of disasters—including an explosion and fire—on the former; and had been dismissed with a bad recommendation by the drunken master of the latter. He had been injured by a flying spar on the *Highland Forest*; had resigned from the *Vidar* and from the *Otago*. Conrad had commanded an ocean-going vessel in Eastern waters. But now, under adverse conditions, he had to seek humble employment as captain of a decrepit, fifteen-ton, fresh-water steamer—which he called "a sluggish beetle"—on an uncharted and perilous river in the middle of Africa.

The Fascination with Africa

In boyhood Conrad's favorite subject was geography. He was thrilled by poring over maps and reading about the African expeditions of Mungo Park on the Niger, James Bruce in Abyssinia, Richard Burton and John Speke in Central Africa. At ten years old, he had looked at a map of Africa, put his finger on the blank space that represented "the unsolved mystery of that continent" and vowed to himself "with absolute assurance and an amazing audacity . . . When I grow up I shall go *there*."

The enormous publicity generated by the more recent adventures of the British explorer and journalist, Henry Morton Stanley, continued to stimulate Conrad's interest in the heart of darkness. . . .

Adolf Krieger's firm, Barr Moering, put Conrad in touch with ship brokers in Ghent [Belgium]. They recommended him, as a man with excellent testimonials, a superior education and the manners of a perfect gentleman, to Albert Thys, the powerful director of the Société Belge pour le Commerce du Haut-Congo. In November 1889 Thys, who gave Conrad the impression of "pale plumpness in a frock coat," interviewed him in Brussels, tested his French (an important qualification for this position) and held out vague possibilities for the future. . . .

Securing a Position

Conrad left the Ukraine, after a two-month visit, on April 18. Eleven days later he reached Brussels and found that a chance event required his immediate presence in the Congo. A Danish captain, Johannes Freiesleben, had, during a trivial quarrel, been murdered by Africans, and Conrad was hired to replace him—as he had been hired in Bangkok to replace the dead master of the *Otago*. In July 1891, the *Official Bulletin* of the Congo reported Freiesleben's death and promised harsh retaliation: "The only really troubled situation was in the region of Tchumbiri, at Bolobo [north of Kinshasa]. In the face of the persistent ill-will and acts of aggression culminating in the assassination of the captain of one of the steamers of the Société du Haut-Congo, over a year ago, it has been necessary to make an example. The security of the white man demands that outrages of this kind be vigorously repressed."

Conrad described his frantic rush back and forth across the [English] Channel in an effort to gather his equipment and say goodbye to his friends before leaving for Africa on May 10. . . .

Conrad signed a three-year contract—his longest commitment to any job—and took the manuscript of *Almayer's Folly* with him to the Congo, but conditions there were not conducive to literary composition.

The Change in View on Colonialism

From 1865 until 1908 the Congo was not a possession of the state of Belgium, but the private property of King Leopold II. Eager for work and inexperienced in Africa, Conrad at first believed the high-minded progaganda about bringing the benevolent light of civilization to the dark continent. Only after he had reached the Congo and seen the brutal exploitation of the resources and the people did he realize it was "the vilest scramble for loot that ever disfigured the history of human conscience and geographical exploration." *The Inheritors* (1901), a novel Conrad wrote with Ford Madox Hueffer (who later changed his surname, and is best known as Ford Madox Ford), satirized Leopold II as the greedy and unscrupulous Duc de Mersch. . . .

Casualties Among Company Employees

After talking to some old Africa hands on the ship, Conrad sent a letter from Freetown, filled with statistics that revealed the alarming rate of casualties: "What makes me rather uneasy is the information that 60 per cent. of our Company's employees return to Europe before they have completed even six months' service. Fever and dysentery! There are others who are sent home in a hurry at the end of a year, so that they shouldn't die in the Congo. . . . In a word, there are only 7 per cent. who can do their three years' service. . . ."

The Influence of Reformer Roger Casement

After a month's voyage, Conrad reached Boma on June 12. The next day he steamed up to Matadi, the farthest navigable point of the Lower Congo, and met the extraordinary Roger Casement, the only man in Africa he was to like and respect. Casement was born in Dublin in 1864. Like Conrad's, his parents died when he was a child; he was brought up by an uncle in northern Ireland, and educated at Ballymena Academy. He became a clerk in a Liverpool trading company when he was

Joseph Conrad in 1904, not long after the publication of Heart of Darkness. © George C. Beresford/Hulton Archive/Getty Images.

eighteen; two years later, in 1884, he sailed for Africa and served King Leopold's Congo Free State as a hunter, explorer, surveyor and administrator. He returned to England after five years of service, but was sent out again the following year to arrange transport for the Belgian authorities on the Lower Congo. In his diary of June 13, Conrad recorded with considerable enthusiasm his meeting with the cultured and experienced Casement: "Made the acquaintance of Mr. Roger Casement, which I should consider as a great pleasure under any circumstances and now it becomes a positive piece of luck. Thinks, speaks well, most intelligent and very sympathetic. . . ."

Conrad shared a room with Casement, who was considered a rather enigmatic personality, for two weeks and soon became very friendly with him. "He knew the coast languages well," Conrad told the Irish-American patron of the arts, John Quinn. "I went with him several times on short expeditions to hold 'palavers' with neighbouring village-chiefs. The object of them was procuring porters for the company's caravans from Matadi to . . . Kinchassa." Writing in 1903 to his swashbuckling anti-imperialist friend, Cunninghame Graham, Conrad described Casement's careless courage and his habit of traveling unarmed and unattended through the dangerous jungle. . . .

Conrad's amazed account of Casement's serene stroll through the unspeakable wilderness suggests that he may have been the model for the elusive and inexplicable Russian in motley in *Heart of Darkness*. On June 28 Conrad trekked upriver to take command of his "tin-pot steamboat" and "parted with Casement in a very friendly manner." They did not meet again until 1896, at a dinner of the Johnson Society in London, which had been founded by Conrad's publisher Fisher Unwin. But Casement had a profound impact on Conrad's attitude toward the Congo and on his fictional portrayal of his grim experience in Africa. . . .

Casement's Humanitarian Achievement

Though he had official sanction from the king's government in Brussels, Casement suffered daily obstructions by the officials of the Free State whose very existence was threatened by his inquiries. His detailed record of the atrocities achieved great force through its moderate tone and objective style, which expressed Casement's passionate commitment to the oppressed. In 1908, after the creation of the Congo Reform Association, Casement finally triumphed. World opinion, stirred by his revelations, forced King Leopold to surrender his personal ownership of the Congo, which became a colony of Belgium. A grateful nation paid the King fifty million francs; Casement was rewarded by the British government and made a Commander of the Order of St. Michael and St. George.

Casement's investigation, which helped to extinguish the cruel and exploitative colonialism in the Congo, stands as one of the great humanitarian achievements of [the twentieth] century. Like Conrad, who shared his feeling of moral outrage, Casement was one of the first men to question the Western notion of progress, a dominant idea in Europe from the Renaissance to the Great War [World War I], to attack the hypocritical justification of colonialism and to reveal in documentary form the savage degradation of the white man in Africa.

Casement's "Congo Diary" substantiated the accuracy of the conditions described in *Heart of Darkness*: the chain gangs, the grove of death, the payment in brass rods, the cannibalism and the human skulls on the fence posts. Casement confirms that Conrad did not exaggerate or invent the horrors that provided the political and humanitarian basis for his attack on colonialism. . . .

In one of his last letters, Casement questioned the value of European civilization in terms that echo one of the most important ideas in *Heart of Darkness*. He juxtaposed the brutal colonists with their "savage" victims just as Conrad contrasted the restrained cannibals and the predatory white "pilgrims": Africa "has been 'opened up' (as if it were an oyster) and the Civilizers are now busy developing it with blood and slaying each other, and burning with hatred against me because I think their work is organized murder, far worse than anything the savages did before them." . . .

Physical Ailments from the Congo Trip

On October 23, four days after Conrad left Kinshasa, the Danish Captain Duhst recorded in his diary: "Camped in a negro town, which is called Fumemba. I am in company with an English captain Conrad from the Kinshasa Company: he is continually sick with dysentery and fever." In *A Personal Record*, confusing Kinshasa and Leopoldville (which are African and Belgian names for the same place), Conrad described the terrible illness that made him quite indifferent to the possible loss of his precious manuscript and to the considerable dangers of the river. He was nearly drowned in

> a specially awkward turn of the Congo between Kinchassa and Leopoldville—more particularly when one had to take it at night in a big canoe, with only half the proper number of paddlers. . . . I got round the turn more or less alive, though I was too sick to care whether I did or not, and, always with *Almayer's Folly* amongst my diminishing baggage, I arrived at the delectable capital Boma, where, before the departure of the steamer which was to take me home I had the time to wish myself dead over and over again with perfect sincerity.

Conrad left Boma for Belgium during the second week in December. After stopping for a few days to see Marguerite [a friend and writer] in Brussels, he reached London on February 1, 1891, and began his dismal convalescence. "When he arrived," Hope recalled, "he looked half dead with fever, so Krieger, who knew the Doctor at the German Hospital at Dalston [in northeast London], got him in there, and he and I used to go see him frequently. The Nurse said she thought he would die, but he pulled round, and in a few weeks was able to go to his rooms, Gillingham Street, near Victoria Station"— his London base for the next six years.

[His uncle] Tadeusz noticed that Conrad's handwriting had greatly changed, and expressed concern about the weakening and exhausting effects of his fever and dysentery. And from the German Hospital, where he spent late February and most of March, Conrad mentioned rheumatism in his left leg, neuralgia in his right arm, swollen veins and legs, thinning hair, as well as disordered nerves, debilitating palpitations of the heart and painful attacks of breathlessness. From May 21 to June 14 he stayed in Champel, a suburb of Geneva, [Switzerland,] at the Hôtel de la Roseraie—a square, four-story building, set in a tree-filled park on the banks of the Arve, with shuttered windows and a balcony with a stone balustrade above the pillared entrance. Here Conrad completed his nervous cure at the Hydropathic Institute by submitting to high-pressure hosings with ice-cold water.

The malarial fever Conrad contracted in the Congo permanently damaged his health. But the psychological effects went even deeper. The long months spent in hospitals and spas allowed him to meditate on his tragic experience and think about how he might transform it into literature. Conrad saw this experience as the turning-point of his intellectual development and once told Edward Garnett: before the Congo, "I was a perfect animal." Afterward, his new insights into the nature of evil turned his innate pessimism into a tragic vision: "I see everything with such despondency—all in black."

Social Issues
in Literature

CHAPTER 2

Heart of Darkness and Colonialism

The Bright Intentions and Dark Realities of Colonialism in *Heart of Darkness*

Albert J. Guerard

Albert J. Guerard, who died in 2000, was a literature professor at Stanford University and a prolific writer of novels and criticism. His subjects included Thomas Hardy and André Gide.

Although Heart of Darkness *is obviously a journey into the self, its commentary on colonialism in the Congo should never be overlooked. The Congo was a frequent topic of discussion in newspapers, journals, and speeches in 1889, when Henry Stanley, the journalist and colonialist working with Belgium's King Leopold, was active.* Heart of Darkness *reveals Joseph Conrad's compassion for the exploited Congolese natives, and he uncovers the cruel hypocrisy of men (like King Leopold) who speak of their forays into Africa as charitable missions but whose only aim is to plunder the area by enslaving the natives. In a place devoid of social restraint, Marlow, unlike Kurtz, is saved by hard work and the power of an inner restraint. Despite Conrad's unequivocal denunciation of colonialism, he seems to have shouldered guilt about working for the colonialists in his brief time in the Congo and in his hope to return—which he never did.*

The autobiographical basis of the narrative [of *Heart of Darkness*] is well known, and its introspective bias obvious; this is Conrad's longest journey into self. But it is well to remember that "Heart of Darkness" is also other if more superficial things: a sensitive and vivid travelogue, and a comment on "the vilest scramble for loot that ever disfigured the history of human conscience and geographical exploration."

Albert J. Guerard, "The Journey Within," *Conrad the Novelist*, Cambridge, MA: Harvard University Press, 1958, pp. 33–38. Reproduced by permission of Collot Guerard.

The Congo was much in the public mind in 1889, when Henry Stanley's relief expedition found Emin Pasha (who like Kurtz did not want to be rescued), and it is interesting to note that Conrad was in Brussels during or immediately after Stanley's triumphant welcome there in April 1890. This was just before he set out on his own Congo journey. We do not know how much the Georges Antoine Klein who died on board the *Roi des Belges* resembled the fictional Kurtz, but Stanley himself provided no mean example of a man who could gloss over the extermination of savages with pious moralisms which were very possibly "sincere."

Marlow's Compassion

"Heart of Darkness" thus has its important public side, as an angry document on absurd and brutal exploitation. Marlow is treated to the spectacle of a French man-of-war shelling an unseen "enemy" village in the bush, and presently he will wander into the grove at the first company station where the starving and sick Negroes withdraw to die. It is one of the greatest of Conrad's many moments of compassionate rendering. The compassion extends even to the cannibal crew of the *Roi des Belges*. Deprived of the rotten hippo meat they had brought along for food, and paid three nine-inch pieces of brass wire a week, they appear to subsist on "lumps of some stuff like half-cooked dough, of a dirty lavender color" which they keep wrapped in leaves. Conrad here operates through ambiguous suggestion (are the lumps human flesh?) but elsewhere he wants ... to make his complacent European reader *see*: see, for instance, the drunken unkempt official met on the road and three miles farther on the body of the Negro with a bullet hole in his forehead. "Heart of Darkness" is a record of things seen and done. But also Conrad was reacting to the humanitarian pretenses of some of the looters precisely as the novelist today [in the late 1950s] reacts to the moralisms of cold-war propaganda. Then it was ivory that poured from the heart of darkness; now it is uranium. Conrad shrewdly recognized—an intuition amply developed in *Nostromo*—that deception is most sinister when it becomes self-deception, and the propagandist takes seriously his own fictions. Kurtz "could get himself to believe anything—anything." The benevolent rhetoric of his seventeen-page report for the International Society for the Suppression of Savage Customs was meant sincerely enough. But a deeper sincerity spoke through his scrawled postscript: "Exterminate all the brutes!" . . .

Conrad, again like many novelists today, was both drawn to idealism and repelled by its hypocritical abuse. "The conquest of the earth, which mostly means the taking it away from those who have a different complexion or slightly flatter noses than ourselves, is not a pretty thing when you look into it too much. What redeems it is the idea only. An idea at the back of it; not a sentimental pretence but an idea; and an unselfish belief in the idea . . . " Marlow commits himself to the yet unseen agent partly because Kurtz "had come out equipped with moral ideas of some sort." Anything would seem preferable to the demoralized greed and total cynicism of the others, "the flabby devil" of the Central Station. Later, when he discovers what has happened to Kurtz's moral ideas, he remains faithful to the "nightmare of my choice." . . . The Kurtz who had made himself literally one of the devils of the land, and who in solitude had kicked himself loose of the earth, burns while the others rot. Through violent not flabby evil he exists in the moral universe even before pronouncing judgment on himself with his dying breath. A little too much has been made, I think, of the redemptive value of those two words—"The horror!" But none of the company "pilgrims" could have uttered them. . . .

Work and Restraint

"Heart of Darkness" (still at this public and wholly conscious level) combines a Victorian ethic and late Victorian fear of the white man's deterioration with a distinctly Catholic psychology. We are protected from ourselves by society with its laws and its watchful neighbors, Marlow observes. And we are protected by work. "You wonder I didn't go ashore for a howl and a dance? Well, no—I didn't. Fine sentiments, you say? Fine sentiments, be hanged! I had no time. I had to mess about with white-lead and strips of woolen blanket helping to put bandages on those leaky steam-pipes." But when the external restraints of society and work are removed, we must meet the challenge and temptation of savage reversion with our "own inborn strength. Principles won't do." This inborn strength appears to include restraint—the restraint that Kurtz lacked and the cannibal crew of the *Roi des Belges* surprisingly possessed. The hollow man, whose evil is the evil of *vacancy*, succumbs. And in their different degrees the pilgrims and Kurtz share this hollowness. "Perhaps there was nothing within" the manager of the Central Station. "Such a suspicion made one pause—for out there there were no external checks." . . .

Guilt About Complicity

In any event, it is time to recognize that the story is not primarily about Kurtz or about the brutality of Belgian officials but about Marlow its narrator. To what extent it also expresses the Joseph Conrad a biographer might conceivably recover, who in 1898 still felt a debt must be paid for his Congo journey and who paid it by the writing of this story, is doubtless an insoluble question. I suspect two facts (of a possible several hundred) are important. First, that going to the Congo was the enactment of a childhood wish associated with the disapproved childhood ambition to go to sea, and that this belated enactment was itself profoundly disapproved, in 1890, by the uncle and guardian. It was another gesture of a man bent on throwing his life away. But even more important may be the guilt of complicity, just such a guilt as many novelists of the Second World War have been obliged to work off. What Conrad thought of the expedition of the Katanga Company of 1890–1892 is accurately reflected in his remarks on the "Eldorado Exploring Expedition" of "Heart of Darkness": "It was reckless without hardihood, greedy without audacity, and cruel without courage . . . with no more moral purpose at the back of it than there is in burglars breaking into a safe." Yet Conrad hoped to obtain command of the expedition's ship even after he had returned from the initiatory voyage dramatized in his novel. Thus the adventurous Conrad and Conrad the moralist may have experienced collision. But the collision, again as with so many novelists of the second [world] war, could well have been deferred and retrospective, not felt intensely at the time.

Victorian Ethics, the New Science, and Colonialism in *Heart of Darkness*

Ian Watt

A distinguished writer and literary critic, Ian Watt, who died in 1999, authored The Rise of the Novel.

Joseph Conrad did not find colonialism a simple issue. He held traditional Victorian values but at the same time became suspicious that those values had been tainted. One of those values was progress, which encouraged colonialism and resulted in the greed that poisoned the colonizers. Colonialism was also enabled by the new Darwinian theory of natural selection, which was applied to society by social philosopher Herbert Spencer with the concept of "the survival of the fittest." Colonialism became focused on Africa, and England and France began fighting each other for control of the continent.

Conrad's first description of *Heart of Darkness* makes it clear that he conceived it in an ideological context: "The *idea* in it," he wrote to William Blackwood, "is not as obvious as in *youth*—or at least not so obviously presented. . . . The criminality of inefficiency and pure selfishness when tackling the civilizing work in Africa is a justifiable idea." This letter was written very early, and refers only to the story's obvious anti-colonial theme; but there are many other ideas in *Heart of Darkness*, which is Conrad's nearest approach to an ideological summa [summation].

That summa emerges from the conflict between Marlow, in whom Conrad the seaman presents his lingering wish to

Ian Watt, "Heart of Darkness," *Conrad in the Nineteenth Century*. Berkeley: University of California Press, 1979, pp. 148–149, 155–160. Reproduced by permission of University of California Press via Copyright Clearance Center.

endorse the standard values of the Victorian ethic, and Kurtz, in whom Conrad the seer expresses his forebodings that the accelerating changes in the scientific, political, and spiritual view of the world during the last decades of the old century were preparing unsuspected terrors for the new.

Marlow's Victorian Ethic

Conrad had arrived in England during the last years of the ascendancy of the Victorian world order. That order, as we can now see more clearly, had essentially been a rearguard action against the destructive implications of the most characteristic new features of nineteenth-century civilisation: the growth of science, industrialism, utilitarianism, democracy, socialism, and individualism. But for a long time a host of optimistic rationalisations were used to conceal the fundamental challenges which the new intellectual and social forces posed to traditional values. Neither Conrad nor Marlow had any faith in the rationalisations, but they adhered to many of the values.

During the late fifties, John Stuart Mill, in his essay on "The Utility of Religion," found it to be characteristic of "an age of weak beliefs" that "such belief as men have" should be "much more determined by their wish to believe than by any mental appreciation of evidence." Conrad's past had bequeathed him this same wish to believe in defiance of all the evidence; and this had led him to adopt a fairly conscious dualism of attitudes. . . .

Colonialism and the Religion of Progress

In the last half of the nineteenth century it was not the physical but the biological sciences which had the deepest and the most pervasive effect upon the way man viewed his personal and historical destiny. The outcry against [naturalist Charles] Darwin's *On the Origin of Species, by Means of Natural Selection, or The Preservation of Favoured Races in the Struggle for Life* (1859) was partly caused by the idea that the species of plants and animals were the accidental products of natural selection and not of a special creation by God as the book of Genesis had it. . . .

This evocation of primordial human history is part of Conrad's reflection of a wider, though indirect, aspect of evolutionary theory in *Heart of Darkness*. Many political and social theorists were fervid believers in what may be called the Victorian religion of progress. Long before Darwin, the traditional view of man's supremacy in the divine plan had been replaced with the idea that an equivalently splendid status could be attained through the working-out of humanity's secular destiny. . . .

The Process of Social Evolution

As regards economic and political matters there developed a loose body of beliefs that became known as Social Darwinism. Darwin himself, though not wholly consistent, had doubted whether any political or social deductions could be drawn from his theories; but Herbert Spencer, who had already introduced the word "evolution" into general currency in 1854, warmly welcomed *The Origin of Species* because it helped fill out his own grand system of the progressive development of every part of the universe—from the stars to the plants. Spencer applied the biological analogy for the sociological part of his scheme; he asserted in *First Principles* (1862), that the "Survival of the Fittest," a term which Darwin later accepted as "more accurate" than natural selection, was a law which validated the current competitive economic order and its attendant inequities, because they were a necessary stage in the process of social evolution.

The same mode of evolutionary argument also supported the ideology of colonial expansion. Merely by occupying or controlling most of the globe, the European nations had demonstrated that they were the fittest to survive; and the exportation of their various economic, political and religious institutions was therefore a necessary step towards a higher form of human organisation in the rest of the world. It was also widely thought—by Spencer, for example—that the dominance of the white races was itself the result of inherited superiority. . . .

In the eighties, public interest in the Empire was spurred on by the discovery of gold in the Transvaal [South Africa], and by increasing resentment at German imperial expansion. The final adoption of an imperialist programme as British government policy occurred when the leadership of the Liberal party passed from William Gladstone to [the Earl of] Rosebery in 1894, and especially when the Conservative ministry of Lord Salisbury took office the next year, with Joseph Chamberlain as colonial secretary. There followed a number of collisions among the great powers over the division of Africa, culminating in the Jameson Raid of 1895, and the Fashoda Incident in 1898, when the French attempt to link their African territories from east to west by establishing a claim to part of the Sudan was turned back by [General Herbert] Kitchener.

Colonial Propaganda and Conrad's Conflict

It was in this atmosphere of intensifying international conflict over Africa, and the consequent spread of jingoist [extreme nationalist] fervour in England, that Conrad wrote *Heart of Darkness*. The new enthusiasm for empire had been fostered by a small group of writers, of whom the most popular was Rider Haggard and the most famous, Rudyard Kipling. Kipling . . . was already the established poet laureate of empire, and the chief propagandist for the values which the imperial mission required—group duty, military discipline, and technological efficiency. Kipling's preoccupation with "The Law" is not unlike Conrad's with solidarity; but although Conrad's seaman values might seem to place him on the side of Kipling, he did not really belong there. Conrad's closest friends

Charles Darwin, the British naturalist who developed the theory of evolution by natural selection. His theories were sometimes applied to the ideals of colonialism. © Time Life Pictures/Mansell/Time and Life Pictures/Getty Images.

were fervid anti-imperialists. . . . Conrad's attitude was divided, and, like many historians, his novels present as many "imperialisms" and "colonialisms" as there are particular cases. In so far as these cases had the common element of conquering, killing, and enslaving the native population, Conrad was opposed, if only because of what had happened to his own native country. He had been dubious about the British forward movement in Africa at the time of the British occupation of Egypt in 1882; and he hoped for a Spanish victory in the 1898 Spanish-American War. But Conrad's commitment to his adopted country brought him into conflict with these sentiments, especially when the Boer War broke out in October 1899. . . .

Although Conrad probably thought that *Blackwood's* [magazine, for which he wrote] would have been unhappy if he made any overt criticism of British imperialism, it is unlikely that he wished to do so. We must not forget that in the nineteenth century no real political alternative had been suggested to Western penetration of the other continents; the only practical issue was what form it should take. The ultimate choice was that which, anticipating Kurtz, a witness before the parliamentary committee on aborigines had expressed as early as 1837: "The main point which I would have in view would be trade, commerce, peace, and civilization. The other alternative is extermination; for you can stop nowhere."

Conrad was equally complicated in his attitude to the ideas of racial superiority which were widely promulgated during the later phases of Anglo-Saxon and German imperialism. . . . Conrad habitually uses the derogatory racial terms which were general in the political and evolutionary thought of his time. This might pose a serious problem if *Heart of Darkness* were essentially concerned with the colonial and racial issue in general. But it is not. As in his earlier Malayan fiction, and in "An Outpost of Progress," Conrad was primarily concerned with the colonisers, and there the general purport of his fiction is consistent and unequivocal: imperial or colonial experience is disastrous for the whites; it makes them lazy; it reveals their weaknesses; it puffs them up with empty vanity at being white; and it fortifies the intolerable hypocrisy with which Europeans in general conceal their selfish aims. . . .

Conrad and Belgian Colonialism

The Belgian Congo, however, provided Conrad with a case where he could speak with absolute freedom, because it was neither British nor a threat to Britain's power in the world, and because the issues involved went far beyond those of race. The colony was ideal for another reason: unlike most others, it had been a conscious creation from the beginning, and a creation accompanied by a deafening international chorus mouthing the moral slogans of evolutionary political progress; but by 1898 this chorus was attacking the savagery of that same [Belgian king] Leopold whom, in 1890, Stanley had called the "Royal Founder of this unique humanitarian and political enterprise."

The inconsistencies in Conrad's attitudes to colonial and racial problems must in general be understood in their historical context: and those in *Heart of Darkness* are particularly influenced by the fact that it was written at a time when Britain had committed herself to stopping further French and German expansion in Africa, even at the risk of war. But *Heart of Darkness* is not essentially a political work; Conrad mainly followed his own direct imaginative perceptions; and insofar as he treated the Africans at all, it was essentially as human beings seen from the inward and subjective point of view which characterises *Heart of Darkness* as a whole.

This emerges from what is perhaps Conrad's most explicit statement on what Belgian colonisation meant for the Africans. He expressed it in a letter of 21 December 1903 to his friend Roger Casement, who was then writing his report on atrocities in the Congo. Conrad wished Casement every success in his campaign; he wondered how a civilisation which at home punishes its citizens for overworking a horse can allow "the moral clock" to be "put back many hours" in the Congo State; and he then gave the moral essence of the problem as he saw it:

[The black man] shares with us the consciousness of the universe in which we live—no small burden. Barbarism per se is no crime . . . and the Belgians are worse than the seven plagues of Egypt insomuch that in that case it was a punishment sent for a definite transgression; but in this the . . . man is not aware of any transgression, and therefore can see no end to the infliction. It must appear to him very awful and mysterious; and I confess that it appears so to me too.

Conrad Was Neither a Colonialist nor a Racist

D.C.R.A. Goonetilleke

D.C.R.A. Goonetilleke is a Conrad scholar and professor emeritus at the University of Kilaniya in Sri Lanka. He has also taught at Cambridge University.

In writing Heart of Darkness, *Joseph Conrad proves to be neither a colonialist nor a racist. Henry Morton Stanley, who was reported to have shot and kicked natives to death and promoted colonialism and King Leopold of Belgium, was one of the models for the murderous Kurtz. Traditional literary critics tended to ignore the issues of colonialism and race, or even suggested that the natives were to blame. But, although the novel came out of a time of colonial enthusiasm and blatant racism,* Heart of Darkness *shows how empty the idea of colonialism is. The overt cruelty described cannot be ignored: in Kurtz's report that ends, "Exterminate all the brutes," and the barbarism that leaves Marlow "horror-struck." Despite Marlow's use of the "N-word" and his failure to develop the native culture, he stresses that the only difference between "them and us" is the circumstances in which we find ourselves.*

It was Henry Morton Stanley's phrases, "the Dark Continent" and "the immense heart of Africa," that passed into general parlance and that figure in Conrad, and the adventurer appears to have indeed been very much a presence behind *Heart of Darkness*; he may well be one of the models for Conrad's portrayal of Kurtz. The brash young American reporter had made his reputation by "finding" [missionary

D.C.R.A. Goonetilleke, "Introduction," in *Heart of Darkness*, Ontario, Canada: Broadview Literary Texts, 1999, pp. 11–18, 20–25. Copyright © 1999 by D.C.R.A. Goonetilleke. Reprinted by permission of Broadview Press.

David] Livingstone in 1871; his many subsequent African involvements were considerably less savoury. His first Congo journey, made at the urging of Leopold II, was an exploration in 1875–77, westwards from Lake Victoria in search of a way to the Atlantic via the Lualaba [River]. At terrible cost both to himself and his party he discovered that the Lualaba became the Congo, and he followed it to the sea; he also established relations with Tippu Tip, a trader in ivory and slaves from Zanzibar who was soon to become the most powerful figure in Central Africa. This was a key voyage in opening up Central Africa to the Europeans, but Stanley's triumph was tainted (as much of his future behaviour would be) by accusations that he was prone to mistreat the native population. At various times he was accused of shooting natives and even of kicking them to death, of attacking defenceless villages, of countenancing looting, of collusion with the slave trade, and of a range of other crimes. Dr. John Kirk, the British Consul at Zanzibar, reported that the 1877 expedition had been "a disgrace to humanity," and Stanley's own words do little to reassure doubters. His many accounts of his expeditions are filled with discussions of appropriate punishments to be inflicted on natives, and he writes in his *Autobiography* of how when his blood was up he would pursue Africans

> up to their villages; I skirmish in their streets, drive them pell-mell into the woods beyond, and level their ivory temples; with frantic haste I fire the huts, and end the scene by towing the canoes to mid-stream and setting them adrift.

By 1878 he had been taken on in Leopold's employ, having helped to convince the Belgian king of what he had been unable to convince his fellow Britons: the Congo could be an enormous source of profit for the European. Between 1879 and 1885 Stanley was the chief figure behind the "development" of the Congo for the Belgians. . . .

Heart of Darkness, Imperialism, and Race

Conrad's Congo journey took place at the high tide of imperialism and racism in European history. It was a period of high-flown ideals as to the supposed "civilizing" influence of European civilization—and a period in which it would not have occurred to many Europeans to think of non-whites in terms of words other than "savage" and "nigger." Even those who were among the most enlightened on such issues held some views that are likely to strike modern readers as condescending; indeed, they may sometimes seem to resemble the outright racists of their day in finding the native peoples of Africa or of Asia "backward" or "childlike." Perhaps the central difference is that for the one group the differences were thought to be built in; Africans were inherently backward, were in their very *essence* "no better than animals." The more enlightened, by contrast, felt that the perceived backwardness was merely a product of circumstance—that in other circumstances, with education and so on, native peoples of the world could become just as "enlightened" as themselves. The essentialist view was the foundation for racist brutality, whereas the anti-essentialist view (ethnocentric though it unquestionably was) laid the path for progress away from imperialist oppression, and indeed away from racism of any sort. . . .

Overlooking Colonialism and Race

The book *is* in important ways about imperialism and racism, and these issues must not be brushed aside. This may seem an obvious truth, but it has not always been recognised. While most of the early reviews treated the text at least in part as a commentary on imperialism, and Belgian imperialism in particular (most, though not all feeling that it presented an attitude highly critical of European behaviour), several laid these themes entirely to one side; it was this second critical tendency that took hold in Conrad criticism as the century moved forward. For generations an exclusively white community of literary critics treated a variety of thematic and stylistic issues (often with great subtlety and insight) while largely ignoring *Heart of Darkness* as a commentary on imperialism or racism. As recently as the 1970s the most influential North American textbook anthology, *The Norton Anthology of English Literature*, summarized *Heart of Darkness* in this fashion:

> In *Heart of Darkness* he draws on his Congo River experience to create an atmosphere of darkness and horror in the midst of which the hero recognises a deep inner kinship with the corrupt villain, the Belgian trader who has lost all his earlier ideals to succumb to the worst elements in the native life he had hoped to improve.

Not only does this summary skim over the appalling oppression of the native population by Kurtz and the imperialist system, but it even appears to blame the natives (in very much the same way as some of the less attractive early reviews did) for the evil that Kurtz perpetrates. Notice in this connection the word "succumb"; it is hard to avoid the connotation that somehow the natives are partly to blame, as if they were somehow holding out temptations to Kurtz. One might almost imagine from this summary that Kurtz is as much victim as villain. . . .

Today even those critics who feel that the most important meanings of the text may concern the souls of individuals, or may concern the heart of humanity as a whole rather than anything connected with Africa or with race, must nevertheless recognise that the text emerges out of the very centre of racism and imperialism, and that no matter how much it may say on one level about humanity as a whole, at another level it has much to say about the treatment of black Africans by white Europeans. As much as it may say something about individuals it also says something about groups; as much as it says something symbolic it also says something about the palpably real. Let us turn, then, to the text itself.

It is significant that the darkness we are first introduced to is not in Africa, but in England. That in Britain's past and present history and in all imperial ventures there is an exploration of darkness is the suggestion in Marlow's opening words: "And this also has been one of the dark places of the earth." The suggestion is elaborated in Marlow's comparison of the Roman Empire and contemporary empires—a comparison which recalls one made by Stanley, but which introduces an irony absent in Stanley in Conrad's treatment of "light" and "darkness." Conrad goes on to suggest that white men have turned the map of Africa into a Dark Continent—thus inverting the conventional view of the Europeans as the harbingers of light. (Later in the tale, Kurtz's painting may be taken to intimate the same inversion of roles.)

Colonialism as an Empty Idea

It is only when we have before us an image of Britons at the receiving end of colonialism that we are offered Marlow's harsh truths and brutal ironies about the present imperialist venture. The structure of the narrative has already reinforced the anti-essentialist sentiment: there is no essential difference between Britons and Congolese other than that the latter have "a different complexion and slightly flatter noses":

> But these chaps were not much account, really. They were no colonists; their administration was merely a squeeze, and nothing more, I suspect. They were conquerors, and for that you want only brute force—nothing to boast of, when you have it, since your strength is just an accident arising from the weakness of others. They grabbed what they could get for the sake of what was to be got. It was just robbery with violence, aggravated murder on a great scale, and men going at it blind—as is very proper for those who tackle a darkness. The conquest of the earth, which mostly means the taking it away from those who have a different complexion or slightly flatter noses than ourselves, is not a pretty thing when you look into it too much. What redeems it is the idea

55

only. An idea at the back of it; not a sentimental pretence but an idea; and an unselfish belief in the idea—something you can set up, and bow down before, and offer a sacrifice to. . . .

It is difficult for the modern reader here to be sure of the degree to which Marlow's "as is very proper for those who tackle a darkness" is to be taken "straight" or as brutal sarcasm. Is the irony here Marlow's, or Conrad's? And to the modern reader it seems incomprehensible that any idea could redeem such barbarity; but, . . . imperialism *was* of course "justified" time and again not as murder and theft but as "something higher." What *Heart of Darkness* shows with subtlety but with devastating clarity is just how vague and how empty the Idea was. Its central expression is in Kurtz's report for the International Society for the Suppression of Savage Customs: seventeen pages of high-flown phrases, of "burning noble words" that "appeal to every altruistic sentiment" . . . "though difficult to remember you know." There was no practical advice whatsoever to interrupt the "magic current of phrases"—or almost none: the sole "practical hint," as Marlow sarcastically terms it, is the "valuable postscriptum" scrawled in an unsteady hand at the foot of the final page, the appalling revelation of the naked racist brutality at the heart of Kurtz and the heart of imperialism: "Exterminate all the brutes!" That is perhaps the ultimate expression of the essentialist extreme in imperialism: "they" are "brutes," different from "the civilized" in every essential quality, irredeemable and expendable. . . .

An Indictment of Imperialism

From here on we are given a continuing litany of appalling human acts. In vivid detail Conrad brings out the suffering caused by imperialism to Africans. They are tortured, killed, exploited, dehumanized in almost every conceivable respect. In the grove of death black men have been reduced by the ravages of disease and starvation to "black shapes," "bundles of acute angles." The manner in which the text presents these images suggests vividly the extent to which the natives have been dehumanized by the brutal treatment they have received—but the distancing mechanisms make the horror that the images call up more vivid rather than less so. Far from the portrayal "glorifying" this dehumanization, both pity and horror are palpably present; Marlow describes his own reaction as being "horror-struck," and it would be an extraordinary reader who did not share the feeling. . . .

It would be hard to imagine a more damning indictment of imperialism than the litany of horrors that are perpetrated here by the Europeans. The effect is to undermine for the reader the sort of imperialistic discourse—"civilizing influence," "blood-thirsty natives," "light-bringers" and so on—that today has long ceased to be taken seriously but that in Conrad's time was almost universally accepted at face value. Indeed, it is a remarkable indicator of the power of ingrained prejudice that although most contemporary reviewers read *Heart of Darkness* as "a criticism of Belgian colonialism," a minority were able to convince themselves that it should not "be supposed that Mr. Conrad makes attack upon colonisation, expansion, even upon Imperialism." . . .

The Noble Savage

It would be foolish to deny, on the other hand, that traces of condescension may be discernible from time to time in the text, as it would be foolish to suggest that the text at any time takes on the viewpoint of the native blacks. We have already seen that the view of native peoples presented in the text occasionally partakes of the idealized "Noble Savage," And unquestionably Marlow shares the tendency common even among the most "enlightened" Europeans to assume that the operation of the mind of the semi-educated African was always influenced by superstition:

He was useful because he had been instructed; and what he knew was this—that should the water in that transparent thing disappear, the evil spirit inside the boiler would get angry through the greatness of his thirst, and take a terrible vengeance.

Marlow—and perhaps Conrad—sees the native Africans as at a stage of culture through which his own race had passed. At a time when the view of history was melioristic [progressively getting better], inevitably he saw Africa as the childhood of human history—childhood being given to whirling, howling, strong griefs and rages, but neither condemned nor condoned. . . .

Contrast the way in which the fireman and the helmsman are presented with the glow that is cast over the original image we are shown of Africans free from European influence and control. A key phrase employed to describe imperialism in the tale is "fantastic invasion"—"invasion," with its connotations of forcible, wrongful intrusion, and displacement. When the text does portray the Africans as primitive, it also suggests that they are best left to themselves—that the white man should not be in Africa. Perhaps the worst fate for the black African, the text seems to suggest, is to obtain only a little of the "white man's learning"—to become like Marlow's fireman, "a dog in a parody of breeches," ironically called "an improved specimen," a hybrid product of two cultures. . . .

Readers today should be careful to see . . . narrative details in the context of the time. . . . Whereas to us it seems inappropriate to downplay resistance to oppression on the part of black Africans, at the time Conrad was writing any suggestions of "aggression" by blacks could be—and were—taken as justification for further oppression. . . .

Marlow is able to imagine the tables turned, the roles of blacks and whites reversed:

The population had cleared out a long time ago. Well, if a lot of mysterious niggers armed with all kinds of fearful weapons suddenly took to travelling on the road between Deal and Gravesend [in England], catching the yokels right and left to carry heavy loads for them, I fancy every farm and cottage thereabouts would get empty very soon. Only here the dwellings were gone, too.

It is almost impossible for the modern reader not to be brought up short by the word "nigger" in this passage. We almost have to force ourselves to go beyond the understanding we now have of the racist connotations of the word to understand what the sentence as a whole is saying: "no wonder these people are making themselves scarce; we would too if they had invaded our country in the way we have invaded theirs and were treating us in the fashion we are treating them." Once again the anti-essentialist attitude is plain; the difference between "them" and "us" is purely one of circumstance.

The Evils of Colonialism's Petty Bureaucracy

Michael Levenson

Michael Levenson, a professor of English at the University of Virginia, has written on Henry James, T.S. Eliot, and James Joyce.

Joseph Conrad's 1898 letter to Blackwood's Magazine, which planned to publish Heart of Darkness, *indicates that his original narrative was primarily a social and political critique of the abusive methods and effects of colonialism or what he described as the "inefficiency" and greed of the "civilizing" work in Africa. Part one of the work is based on factual history, Conrad's actual experiences. His early conception of Kurtz's role was simply as an example and symbol of the "insidious" corruption of imperialism. This changed somewhat. It is the manager who is the epitome of the rivalry, incompetence, and power to create identities and destinies. Kurtz, who is somehow above this pettiness, still illustrates how lofty intentions (his early commitment to "civilize" the natives) differ from malicious actions (his tyranny over the tribe).*

In a letter to William Blackwood dated 31 December 1898, Conrad refers to a new story that he is preparing for *Blackwood's Magazine,* "a narrative after the manner of *Youth*" that is already "far advanced." He discloses his working title, *The Heart of Darkness* but quickly adds that "the narrative is not gloomy. The criminality of inefficiency and pure selfishness when tackling the civilizing work in Africa is a justifiable idea." He remarks that "the subject is of our time distinctly"

Michael Levenson, "The Value of Facts in *Heart of Darkness*," *Nineteenth-Century Fiction*, vol. 40, no. 3, December 1985, pp. 261–264, 266–270, 275–276. Reproduced by permission of University of California Press via Copyright Clearance Center.

and compares it to "my *Outpost of Progress*," noting, however, that the new work is "a little wider—is less concentrated upon individuals." . . .

The Political Question

During the first week of January he completes the portion of the story that will ultimately become the first installment of the published work and that conforms well to the initial outline offered to Blackwood. The bitter evocation of imperialism merits the description "of our time," and the rapidly shifting attention among characters and incidents explains why Conrad thought of his story as somewhat diffuse. This early section, as carefully managed as it is, nevertheless remains within the relatively humble boundaries that Conrad had mentioned, a kind of *Youth*-cum-"An Outpost of Progress" in which the agency of Marlow is brought to bear upon the Social Question. . . .

Part One not only emphasizes the political question; it stays close to the historical facts. Conrad draws heavily on events he had witnessed; and given the initial statements to Blackwood, it is highly likely that he first projected the tale as a reasonably faithful rendering of the European entanglement in Africa, a series of sordid misadventures culminating in the pointless death of a European trader. Conrad's own experience with the trader Klein remains obscure; we know that Klein was brought aboard the *Roi des Belges* at Stanley Falls and that he died during the trip downriver; but we have no reason to suppose that Conrad's encounter with him bore any significant resemblance to Marlow's uncanny confrontation with Kurtz. Indeed the dissimilarity gives us a way to understand why Conrad thought that he would finish the story so quickly and why he assumed, even when it was well advanced, that it would not go much beyond the present end of Part One. For if he had continued to trace the pattern of his own unpleasant ordeal in the Congo, the meeting with Kurtz would doubtless have been rendered in far more modest terms and would have served more as a pendant to the angry social critique, a final senseless misfortune in a long sequence of unnecessary blunders. . . .

Kurtz Is Colonialism

Halfway through Part One Marlow roundly denounces the European presence in Africa.

> I've seen the devil of violence, and the devil of greed, and the devil of hot desire; but by all the stars! these were strong, lusty, red-eyed devils, that swayed and drove men—men, I tell you. But as I stood on this hillside, I foresaw that in the blinding sunshine of that land I would become acquainted with a flabby, pretending, weak-eyed devil of a rapacious and pitiless folly. How insidious he could be, too, I was only to find out several months later and a thousand miles farther.

The last comment furnishes a second reference to Kurtz's fall, but we should pay careful attention to the context. Speaking from his retrospective standpoint on the *Nellie*, Marlow invokes Kurtz as the most "insidious" manifestation of the "flabby, pretending, weak-eyed devil." And yet "flabby," "pretending" and "weak-eyed" are perhaps the last attributes one would bestow on Kurtz, whose moral descent will far exceed the connotations of "folly." Furthermore, in this early passage Marlow *opposes* the corruption he will meet upriver to the "manly" devils of violence, greed, desire, and lust. But Kurtz, let us recall, will appear precisely as a man who "lacked restraint in the gratification of his various lusts," who indulged "forgotten and brutal instincts," "gratified and monstrous passions."

In other words, this early reference suggests that Kurtz's afflictions will be thoroughly continuous with the criminality of imperialism, that there will be no "choice of nightmares," only one increasingly appalling phantasm. Within this conception Kurtz would pose no distinctly psychological problem; he would represent merely the most extreme, the most "insidious" example of the general corruption. At this point it even remains unclear whether Conrad had anticipated the celebrated motif of voluntary reversion to the primitive. . . .

The Power of the Colonizer

Criticism of the novel has always, and naturally, focused upon the conclusion, that *après* ["after"] which is the fiction's crux. The jungle, the horror, the return, the lie—these no doubt pose the most absorbing problems of the work. But part of our purpose is to see how the opening of the tale engenders its culmination, and if we rush too quickly to the conclusion we miss its motivation and diminish its force. We miss, for one thing, the extent to which *Heart of Darkness* is a drama of officialdom. Imperialism presents itself to Conrad as an affair of inefficient clerks, disaffected functionaries, envious subordinates, and defensive superiors—all arrayed within a strict hierarchy whose local peak is the General Manager and whose summit is the vague "Council in Europe." The Company gives identities, establishes purposes, assigns destinies, and with its bizarre configuration of Central and Inner Stations even constructs geography. The accumulation of ivory is the material goal, but it interests Conrad less than its social consequence, the scramble for position within the institution, which creates its own flabby passions and even its own flabby pentameter: "Am I the manager—or am I not? . . . "

From the perspective of a "value-free" sociology [Max] Weber dispassionately charts the rise of the bureaucratic sensibility, but a detectable bitterness enters his tone, and outside his formal studies it erupts into derision and contempt.

> It is horrible to think that the world could one day be filled with nothing but those little cogs, little men clinging to little

jobs and striving towards bigger ones. . . . This passion for bureaucracy . . . is enough to drive one to despair. . . .

Under the same historical pressures Conrad came to much the same perception. . . .

The Disgusting Bureaucracy of Colonialism

Within this set of concerns the Manager is the exemplary figure, and we simply misread the work if we neglect the importance of this character who typifies the vulgar sensibility of petty officialdom and who incarnates the criminality, inefficiency, and selfishness that Conrad first set out to expose. A man with "no learning, and no intelligence," "neither civil nor uncivil," the Manager "was obeyed, yet he inspired neither love nor fear, nor even respect." He jealously guards "trade secrets," deprecates "unsound method," and coldly submits human welfare to institutional requirements. The epitome of the bureaucrat, he "originated nothing, he could keep the routine going— that's all." In important respects the Manager is the displaced center of *Heart of Darkness* who would have held pride of place in the shorter work that Conrad had first conceived. . . .

Not only the origins of the tale but its structure must be understood in the context of Conrad's revulsion from the bureaucratic sensibility. Kurtz enters the work, and perhaps entered Conrad's imagination as an antithesis to the Manager, as though he were summoned into being through the strength of Conrad's repugnance. Marlow first hears his name from the chief accountant, who describes him as "a first-class agent," and then, noting Marlow's disappointment, adds that Mr. Kurtz "is a very remarkable person." The distinction between "agent" and "person" is fundamental; for in its initial movement the tale dramatizes the attempt to recover personality from a world of impersonal functionaries, an activity that begins within a strictly institutional context. . . . Furthermore, he has "moral ideas"; and when he is still "just a word," Marlow posits him as the ethical alternative to economic privacy.

Heart of Darkness begins, that is, by identifying a bureaucratic conflict, the struggle between the good and the bad official and, by implication, a struggle between moral and immoral forms of social organization.

These, of course, are not the struggles that we ultimately witness. But the transformation in the narrative must be understood against the background of this original problem— the need to find a perspective from which to oppose institutionalized depravity. Kurtz's turn to the wilderness, whatever else it becomes, is first of all a gesture of social rebellion. The Tribe is a rejoinder to the Company. Under Kurtz's domination the Tribe possesses a seamless unity that avoids the endless articulations of bureaucracy; it knows no legal formalism, no reliance on a vague "They, above," whose lofty intentions dissipate in the long descent through hierarchy. For Conrad the inefficiency of imperialism is not one defect among many: it is a measure of the awful distance between intention and action so inimical to coherent social purpose. Within the Tribe authority exists not as a remote official dispatching instructions through the mail but as a visible body and a living voice—a "real presence." The distance between the will and its realization is overcome; inefficiency disappears as a problem; Kurtz makes the canoes run on time. . . .

The Foundation of Morality and Restraint

A perception of the distance between fact and value is fundamental to Conrad's assault on prevailing social conventions. . . . Certainly, a familiar approach to *Heart of Darkness* considers it a rejection of the values of progress and enlightenment in the name of such facts as passion, greed, and violence. But we need to acknowledge a third category of Conradian concepts that is distinct from both the class of groundless ideals and the class of amoral instincts.

During Kurtz's final crisis Marlow watches "the inconceivable mystery of a soul that knew no restraint, no faith, and no fear, yet struggling blindly with itself." Here is Conrad's improbable image for the foundation of morality, an image that locates the moral source not in social convention but in an inconceivably mysterious gesture of the individual mind. Kurtz, a man without restraint, struggles to restrain himself. . . .

When Marlow encounters the unlikely self-control of the hungry cannibals aboard his ship, he stands amazed: "Restraint! I would just as soon have expected restraint from a hyena prowling amongst the corpses of a battlefield." Then he immediately adds, "But there was the fact facing me—the fact dazzling, to be seen, like the foam on the depths of the sea." . . . A notion such as restraint suggests the possibility of a natural basis for ethics, a nonmoral ground for morality, a reconciliation between fact and value.

The Theme of Death in *Heart of Darkness*

Garrett Stewart

A professor of English at the University of Iowa, Garrett Stewart has published Framed Time, Novel Violence, *and* Bookwork.

Colonialism is inevitably a bringer of death, no matter when or where or why it occurs, from ancient Rome to Marlow's day. The women knitting as he leaves the company offices are like "harbingers of death." Death comes to the servants of colonialism (chiefly through disease) as well as to their victims. Two of Marlow's predecessors have died. And Kurtz's gaunt look is a reminder of the skeleton of the agent Marlow finds. Death adheres to both Kurtz, the personification of greed, and to those he has killed. Marlow indicts England when he associates Kurtz with England. Lying in the novel, by white-washing Kurtz and colonialism, is equated with death. In lying to the "Intended" at the last, Marlow undercuts his critical observations and shows that he continues to support the "idea" or "ideal" of European invasion and plunder of Africa, connecting himself to Kurtz.

The plot of *Heart of Darkness* is in part a political autopsy of imperialist myths. A level-headed seaman named Marlow, teller of his own tale, journeys to the Congo as steamer captain for a European trading company; hears rumors about another agent of the company, an eloquent mastermind named Kurtz; later discovers that the man has submitted to, rather than suppressed, the natives' savagery, with its hints of cannibalism and sexual license; finally meets up with Kurtz, remaining by his side to hear the man's deathbed judgment on his own degeneracy and diabolism; and then returns to Eu-

Garrett Stewart, "Lying as Dying in *Heart of Darkness*," *PMLA*, vol. 95, no. 3, May 1980, pp. 319–321, 326–327. Reprinted by permission of the Modern Language Association of America.

rope to lie about Kurtz's "worthy" end in order to give the man's fiancée something to live for and with. Marlow's trek toward Kurtz, first by water, then by land, is made now in the wake of a generalized epidemic of death, now in the footsteps of walking specters: a dead march to the heart of a defunct and festering ideal of European superiority. Though the novel's "adjectival insistence," which so famously annoyed [critic] F.R. Leavis, centers nowhere more relentlessly than on permutations of "dark" and "deadly," "tenebrous" and "moribund," the effect is one not so much of morbid atmospherics as of moral asperity, an attack on death-dealing imperialist motives and the truths they obscure.

Primary Human Impulses

Heart of Darkness harkens back to origins. It suggests that a naked exposure of the human ego, unshielded by civilization and its self-contents, to a world of savagery presumed to be far beneath it is, in the long evolutionary run, only a baring of the soul to the most primally rooted human impulses. To plumb the native is to come up against the innate, apart from all cultural or racial demarcations. Even before Marlow begins his African narrative proper, he ruminates that the Thames [River], on which he and his fellow seamen are traveling, has also been, as far back as the Roman colonization, "one of the dark places of the earth." Apropos of the story to come, this initial sense of a primordial blackness triggers an association, more than gratuitous, with "death skulking in the air, in the water, in the bush. They must have been dying like flies here." In Roman England under the pall of colonization, yes, just as in Africa, where Marlow found everywhere "the merry dance of death and trade . . . in a still and earthly atmosphere as of an overheated catacomb," where trade rivers were "streams of death in life."

Beyond the sinister topography of the African landscape, which lays bare the inevitable brutality of imperialism as itself a mode of death, Marlow has also faced his own private demise in an embodied omen. On leaving the company offices in Europe, he must pass by those black-garbed, knitting women, the sibylline harpies and harbingers of death, to whom departing agents seem to sense as the appropriate valediction "Morituri te salutant" [We who are about to die salute you]. As one about to die, or narrowly to skirt his own death, Marlow shortly after encounters two European predecessors, predeceased, on his way to what he calls (recalling a metaphor from its grave) the "dead center" of Africa. . . .

Death to the Invader and Invaded

Kurtz himself is introduced as the barely living fulfillment of the mortal fate of Marlow as contemplated through his double, Fresleven—though such thoughts hover at the level of mere foreboding, without as yet any explicit parallel between Marlow and Kurtz, except that they are both European agents in Africa. When Kurtz makes his long-delayed appearance Marlow describes him too, like Fresleven, as a skeleton, "the cage of his ribs all astir, the bones of his arms waving". . . . Kurtz as breathing skeleton keeps company with the remains of Fresleven as a death's-head memento mori [reminder of mortality]. As Kurtz emerges from his blankets "as if from a winding-sheet," his moribund condition is also personally retributive, an oblique revenge on himself, as arch imperialist, for those untended dying natives in that "grove of death" Marlow had earlier come on, all of whom were reduced to skeletal "bundles of acute angles." In tandem with this ironic reprisal for Kurtz—the witherer withered—is another symbolic pattern of poetic justice, for Kurtz has also been shriveled to an image of the precious corrupted element, the cold ivory, in which he has traded and debased his humanistic ideals. The mania for this dead bone strikes Marlow from the first as having a "taint of imbecile rapacity" like (as with lying for that matter) "a whiff from some corpse," and when Kurtz appears

Still from Apocalypse Now, *a 1979 film that was inspired by* Heart of Darkness. *Garrett Stewart points out that colonialism brings death to both invaders and their victims.* © Michael Ochs Archives/Getty Images.

on the scene to personify that greed, his all-but-fossilized being seems like "an animated image of death carved out of old ivory."

Disapproval of English Colonialism

Even before Kurtz's first onstage appearance a premature and precipitous description of him as a breathing corpse broke into Marlow's chronological narrative, providing a glimpse of the story's haunted destination. Marlow cannot keep down the need to tell his auditors in advance that the visionary encounter with genius he had gone in search of would never be more than spectral—the eviscerated Kurtz reduced, by the time Marlow first sees him, to a disembodied voice in a "disinterred body." Exploring Marlow's preoccupation with Kurtz *as voice* leads us to recognize the logic of such a premature intrusion, for it argues the deepest logic of the novel's first full-dress death, which frames this premonition, the wordless end of a subtly partial doppelgänger [double] for Marlow and Kurtz together in the former's native helmsman. Marlow can share in Kurtz's slaying self-knowledge because "it"—what was left of the man, his neutered "shade" or "wraith"—"it could speak English to me. The original Kurtz had been educated partly in England." Thus Conrad quietly implicates England, and Marlow as Englishman, in Kurtz's European hubris and diseased idealism—and of course implicates himself, too, as British-educated master of nonnative English eloquence. I introduce Conrad's famed English, not just Marlow's expert story-telling, because the local stress on the risks and responsibilities of rhetorical power seems to broaden outward into a comment on the dark expressiveness that brings us the story in the first place. . . .

Lying Is Dying

Given what we know of Marlow's ultimate attitude toward the Congo experience, the surprise is that criticism can so widely persist in thinking Marlow's whitewashing capitulation merely a white lie, a sacrificial violation of his own spiritual insight out of humanist charity. When he pontificates early on about lie's taint, the point is hammered home as a personal revulsion. Lying "appalls me"; it is "exactly what I hate and detest in the world"; it "makes me miserable and sick, like biting into something rotten would." One must doubt whether it could be simply for the solace of another that he later submits himself to his spiritual death. His strict ethical theorem, the equation of death with lying, is even in the early context no stray remark, for it threads untruth to death in the causal nexus of the European experience in Africa. What dying and lying have in common is that they both induce decay, the psychic moribundity and physical decomposition visible everywhere on that colonized landscape we traverse on our way to the death of Kurtz. The novel's largest lie is the one that premises its experience: the ultimately self-revenging hubris of imperial impulse. The question is what degree of collusion in this untruth Marlow, long its implicit critic, ultimately allows himself to take comfort in.

Marlow's Self-Deception

Against the muddied tide of critical opinion, Eloise Knapp Hay, writing about the political novels of Joseph Conrad, has helped us to see how the political self-deception of Marlow serves to discredit him as a morally reliable narrator. For though we read the novel as a progressive disclosure of European delusions in Africa, we must recall that Marlow's words of introduction are uttered from the vantage of retrospect, uttered and thus undercut. Having seen the darkness at the heart of Europe's colonizing onslaughts, he can still say, with a combination of political acuity and idealistic confusion: "'The conquest of the earth, which mostly means the taking it away from those who have a different complexion or slightly flatter noses than ourselves, is not a pretty thing when you look into it too much. What redeems it is the idea only. An idea at the back of it; not a sentimental pretence but an idea; and an unselfish belief in the idea—something you can set up, and bow down before, and offer a sacrifice to. . . . ' He broke off." Despite his witnessing to the inevitable corruption that comes from white imperialism, Marlow would seem to be saying that without "selfishness" Kurtz could have succeeded, and yet the very claim is demolished by the religious imagery of bowing and sacrificing. Idealism degrades itself to idol worship, as we know from the perverse exaltation and adoration of Kurtz in the jungle, his ascent to godhead.

The inbred spoilage of an ennobling ideal was also sketched out with the first jungle victim we heard about in any detail, the Danish captain Fresleven, who began as "the gentlest, quietest creature that ever walked on two legs." Yet he was murdered by a native while "mercilessly" beating an African chief over some misunderstanding about two black hens. After all, Marlow says without surprise, "He had been a couple of years already out there engaged in the noble cause, you know, and he probably felt the need at last of asserting his self-respect in some way." Thus is the nobility of the white man's grand burden sapped and trivialized. Marlow's parenthetical "you know" (such things taken for granted by us far-thinking Europeans) teeters uneasily between sarcasm and apologetics; Marlow himself is unsure how to feel about his beloved idealism, however fine and selfless, when it can be so readily undermined, here and of course with Kurtz, by eruptions of the ego in sadistic self-assertion. Indeed Kurtz seemed at first the very embodiment of this "noble cause," but too much its incarnation in the long run, too little its acolyte. If Kurtz somewhere held to any glimmer of his original "idea," he must have lost sight of it entirely amid the blackness of his end. Does Marlow mean to imply, however, that Kurtz is the kind of "sacrifice" the idea deserves? Surely Kurtz died in the name of his idea's death, not its perpetuation, died at the hands of his own traitorous neglect of the ideal. There are, Marlow is so far right, purposes in themselves sublime, but when they are implemented by persons in power the danger is always that others will be sacrificed to the ghost of idealism's grandeur, cannibalized by its rhetoric and its personal magnetism. Bowing down, we tend to give up our vigilance. In line with the imagery of adoration, Marlow himself is twice described in the prologue as an inscrutable effigy, first with a posture and complexion that "resembled an idol" and later, just before his defense of imperialism, with "the pose of a Buddha preaching in European clothes and without a lotus-flower." His own person partially incarnates that idolatry masquerading as an almost religious truth—in another key, Kurtz's idealism turned demonic—which is the monitory [cautioning] center of his tale. Though Marlow knows the evils of white suppression at first hand, he represses them far enough from consciousness to leave continued space for the European idealism he still shares with "the original Kurtz."

The Colonizer Becomes the Savage in *Heart of Darkness*

Carola M. Kaplan

Carola M. Kaplan, a professor emerita of English at California State University–Pomona, has published on Joseph Conrad, Henry James, E.M. Forster, and T.E. Lawrence, among others.

Heart of Darkness *contains many polar opposites, including civilization vs. savagery and the Self vs. the Other (or those unlike the self). Marlow records what he does not fully understand; that is, that the lines between these opposites collapse in the course of the narrative. He talks about what seems to be Kurtz's cultural mission to Africa, but then shows the reader the heads on poles around Kurtz's house. In the Intended's elegant, civilized drawing room are repeated echoes of "savage" Africa, including the ivory piano keys. Marlow's stereotypical descriptions of Africans and women are his denial of their humanity, potential power, and identification with him. Those two supposed opposites—the cannibals and the colonizers—become one when the reader realizes that the colonizers have devoured the natives symbolically. Ironically, "the horror" may be the name of his Intended, if one considers her to be a driving force behind colonialism.*

"Man can embody truth but he cannot know it." Nowhere is [poet] William Butler Yeats's adage more clearly illustrated than in the narrative of Charlie Marlow in *Heart of Darkness*. Throughout the text, Marlow insists upon the distinction between truth and lies; between men and women; between civilization and savagery; and, most of all, between Self and Other. Of these, the most important distinc-

Carola M. Kaplan, "Colonizers, Cannibals, and the Horror of Good Intentions in Joseph Conrad's *Heart of Darkness*," *Studies in Short Fiction*, vol. 34, no. 3, Summer 1997, pp. 323–337. Reproduced by permission.

tion is between Self and Other, for it is this opposition that sustains the colonial enterprise. The lure and the fear of the Other initiate the pursuit and "discovery" of colonialism; the conviction of the inferiority of the Other justifies the undertaking. Yet despite Marlow's insistence, all binary oppositions collapse in the course of his narrative: colonists prove to be conquerors, the gang of virtue is indistinguishable from the gang of greed, the illusions of women merely echo the illusions of men, and there is no clear distinction between lies and truth. Most importantly, the fundamental difference between Self and Other disappears and, with it, the unbridgeable gulf between men and women and between savage and civilized that sustains the power structure of western civilization. But this awareness offered by the text eludes Marlow for, enmeshed in his own culture, he would find this awareness "too dark—too dark altogether." . . .

Marlow's Self-Deception

Heart of Darkness points to awarenesses beyond Marlow both by revealing his limitations and by systematically undercutting the polarities and distinctions that Marlow takes pains to establish. From the first, Marlow's narrative invites the reader to reach an understanding beyond him when he states that his experience was "not very clear. And yet it seemed to throw a kind of light." Among his many limitations in dealing with cultural differences, Marlow displays his xenophobia [fear of strangers/foreigners] when he reluctantly accepts his relatives' choice of living on the Continent, explaining, "It's cheap and not so nasty as it looks, they say." Further, he exhibits contradictory ideas about entering another culture, revealing his determination to get to Africa "by hook or by crook" but, once there, feeling like "an imposter" when he observes that the natives (unlike him) "wanted [lacked] no excuse for being there." He insists that he detests and avoids lies, yet acknowledges three separate lies in the course of the narrative—to the station manager, to Kurtz, and to the Intended. He maintains that the conquest of the earth is redeemed by "an unselfish belief in the idea—something you can set up, and bow down before, and offer a sacrifice to." Not only is this assertion undercut by the language of idolatry, but it prefigures evidence, as the narrative unfolds, that Kurtz' belief in the idea of "humanizing, improving, instructing" leads to the most ruthless exploitation and most appalling idolatry of all, as Kurtz turns himself, the emissary of the idea, into an object of worship. Further, Marlow dismisses as foolish his aunt's notion of "weaning those ignorant millions from their horrid ways," but describes as "a beautiful piece of writing" Kurtz' kindred assertion, "By the simple exercise of our will we can exert a power for good [among the natives] practically unbounded." Throughout the text, Marlow works hard to separate savage customs from civilized behavior, yet an observer might be pressed to distinguish Marlow's noisy jig with the boilermaker (when he finally gets rivets to repair his boat) from the "whirl of black limbs" on shore that he condescends to regard as "not inhuman." Similarly, Marlow's distinction between the comprehensible language of civilized discourse and the incomprehensible noise of savages—"the roll of drums," "abrupt burst of yells," "savage clamour," "savage discords," "tumultuous and mournful uproar"—breaks down. All voices, European and native, degenerate in Marlow's memory into "one immense jabber, silly, atrocious, sordid, savage, or simply mean, without any kind of sense". . . .

The Colonialism of the Drawing Room

Many apparently innocent features of the drawing room recall sinister aspects of the colonial enterprise presented earlier in the story. Thus, the grand piano "like a sombre and polished sarcophagus" recalls the image of Brussels, the city outside her door, site of the colonial Company's offices, as "a whited sepulchre"; the piano, symbol of feminine refinement, has keys of ivory, the ivory Kurtz pilfered from Africa; the apparently noble image of the Intended's white forehead "illumined by the unextinguishable light of belief and love" against the dark background of the room recalls Kurtz's ominous painting of her "draped and blindfolded, carrying a torch" in which "the effect of the torch-light on the face was sinister." In the drawing room scene, she is in effect blindfolded by her enduring and willful illusions about Kurtz and she carries the torch of his ideas, which cast a sinister light back upon her. Fittingly, the image of her hair as an "ashy halo" associates her apparently angelic goodness with death. Consequently Marlow, in acknowledging that the Intended's claim, "I knew him best," may be accurate, aptly notes that "with every word spoken the room was growing darker"—that is, more unfathomable, more remote from truth, more connected with evil, more suggestive of death. In this scene all details combine to point out that domestic innocence colludes with global evil in death-dealing conspiracy. Yet, in the Intended's drawing room, as in other stations along his pilgrimage, Marlow shrinks from the enormity of the knowledge he is offered.

Denial of Female and African Power

Similarly, in his descriptions of the African natives, as in his glib generalizations about women, Marlow likewise attempts to deny the power of the Other he fears by resorting to stereotypes. Just as his descriptions of women are reductive, so too are his accounts of the natives, whom he acknowledges only in generic descriptions. "Dark human shapes could be made out in the distance . . . two bronze figures, leaning on tall spears, stood in the sunlight under fantastic head-dresses of spotted skins, warlike and still in statuesque repose." Even when described individually, they are stereotyped: "The man seemed young—almost a boy—but you know with them it's hard to tell." Marlow's stereotypical descriptions of both women and natives serve a strategy of containment that enables him to deny both their importance for him and his affinity with them.

Nowhere, however, is Marlow's containment of the Other through discourse so sustained as in his treatment of the "savage" woman, the figure in which race and gender emblematically intersect. This is not to say that racial and sexual difference are to be equated. Since the value attributed to each is culturally determined, interpretations of racial and sexual superiority vary from one culture to another; and within any particular culture these constructions may conflict rather than intersect. Yet when *Heart of Darkness* presents an African tribal culture that reverses both the racial and sexual hierarchy of the West, these reversals constitute a powerful double threat to Western social constructions that Marlow views as natural and inevitable.

Marlow's compelling but ambivalent description of the "savage" woman enables the reader to see the contrast between her authority and unique attributes and Marlow's repeated attempts, throughout the text, to deny the power and individuality of African natives. Marlow responds to her dangerous allure—dangerous because he sees her as partly responsible for Kurtz's "going native"—by insisting on her ineradicable twofold otherness, the savage and female as distinguished from the civilized and male. By designating her the living embodiment of these dualities, Marlow shores up the binary oppositions upon which his understanding of Western civilization rests. . . .

Colonizers as Cannibals

The cannibalism Marlow imputes to the natives may be merely a guilty projection of the rapacity of the white colonizers who, as [satirist] Jonathan Swift noted about earlier British colonial exploiters in "A Modest Proposal," have already devoured the native population in less literal ways. Since the European in-

Europeans in Congo circa 1900. Carola M. Kaplan argues that European colonizers, who considered themselves civilized, took on the role of savages as they symbolically devoured the African natives. © Hulton Archive/Stringer/Hulton Archive/Getty Images.

truders have invaded territorial boundaries, have violated property rights, and have in fact confiscated the natives' most personal property—their bodies—for their own uses, the Europeans are but one step from literally devouring the inhabitants. In fact, Marlow describes the insatiable Kurtz as threatening to do so: "I saw him open his mouth wide—it gave him a weirdly voracious aspect, as though he had wanted to swallow all the air, all the earth, all the men before him." Even Marlow's approval of the apparent restraint of the natives aboard ship, whom he takes to be hungry cannibals, may simply suggest the guilt he feels at the Europeans' lack of restraint toward the indigenous population. . . .

The African natives exist in the text as expressions of Kurtz's—and Marlow's—intentions. They exist for Kurtz's uses and are confined to Marlow's conceptions of them. To have intentions toward a people is to appropriate for oneself the right to subdue, to convert, and to use—all in the name of benevolence. Thus "the horror" is indeed the name of the Intended: it designates the violence that results from the intentions of the powerful who impose their will upon the powerless. . . .

By the time Marlow tells the truth he considers a lie when he suggests that "the horror" is the name of Kurtz's Intended (that is to say, the name for what he had intended), the text has effectually blurred the distinction between truth and lies, much as it has blurred the distinctions between colonists and conquerors, between savagery and civilization, between men's realities and women's illusions.

If, as has often been claimed, Marlow represents a white, patriarchal, Eurocentric view of late nineteenth-century history, the text suggests, although it does not develop, a perspective on contemporary global politics that is more complex and more problematic than Marlow's. Unlike Marlow's conflation of all historic periods into one universal time and his insistence that Africa mirrors the beginnings of Western civilization, the text marks a specific moment in the European imperialist enterprise, the moment in which late nineteenth-century England, disconcertingly akin to the more overtly ruthless Belgium, was frantically grabbing territory in outlying regions of the world. Unlike Marlow's erasure of class differences through his creation of an artificially egalitarian community aboard a yacht (in which a plain seaman rubs elbows with a lawyer and a director of companies), the text recognizes that even in the jungle class barriers exist between colonial officials and working men, such as mechanics and boiler-makers. . . .

Finally, the narrative stipulates that what it arbitrarily equates with darkness is in fact universal—an ineradicable core of evil in all human beings, whatever their culture of origin. When Marlow observes about modern England, "And this also . . . has been one of the dark places of the earth," his use of the perfect tense brings his observation into the present. By the time Marlow ceases to speak to his audience on the "cruising yawl," symbolically the privileged site of the dominant culture, all persons on board must acknowledge that the apparently "tranquil waterway" of modern European history leads "into the heart of an immense darkness," located not only in the outposts of empire but always already within the human breast.

Marlow Dispels the Illusions About Colonialism

Bernard J. Paris

Bernard J. Paris, English professor emeritus at the University of Florida, has published books on Joseph Conrad, George Eliot, Fyodor Dostoyevsky, and John Milton.

By telling his story of colonialism in the Congo, Marlow is trying to destroy his friends' illusions about the empire. His companions on the Thames River make remarks that seem to glorify colonialism—the "Hunters for gold," soldiers, and "knights-errant" in the history of England. But Marlow sees their views as ludicrous as he compares the ancient Roman conquerors on the Thames River with the colonizers he has encountered on the Congo River. He parallels the rapacious Romans with the "robbery and violence" in Africa. Colonizers like the nineteenth-century Europeans, unlike the conquerors of ancient Rome, express their intention to do good, but their actions show that they are really motivated by greed. And in an unknown place, where colonizers can exercise unlimited power, concern for the good of others is replaced by overweening ego. Marlow starts his adventure as a "romantic individualist," but after seeing the horror of Kurtz's self-absorption, he begins to value the constraints and relationships of society in England.

Far from being a producer of words that cannot be traced to a single personality, Marlow the narrator is an integral part of a highly developed mimetic portrait. Indeed, the telling of his story may be Marlow's most complicated act. He is trying to produce an effect on his audience, but he is also trying to accomplish a number of things for himself. His telling

Bernard J. Paris, "Marlow the Narrator," *Conrad's Charlie Marlow: A New Approach to "Heart of Darkness" and Lord Jim*, New York: Palgrave, 2006, pp. 55–64, 66–67. Reproduced by permission of Palgrave Macmillan.

his story is part of his struggle to grasp the meaning of the Congo experience and to reestablish a conception of existence with which he can live. He is trying to deal with the emotional stress that has been produced by his encounters with unshackled nature, primitive man, and degenerate Europeans. He is still haunted by his relationship with Kurtz and his lie to the Intended. He needs to understand his motivations and to restore his pride. So far, his disturbing experiences seem to have been pent-up inside him. Apparently, he regards his present companions as people to whom he can unburden himself. Marlow has multiple motives for telling his tale, not all of which operate at once. Some are more important at the outset, while others come into play as the story progresses. . . .

A Romanticized View of the Thames

Marlow's initial remarks are prompted by observations on the Thames [River] made by his companions. These observations may have been made by the frame narrator alone or by several members of the company. They are presented in summary form rather than as one or more speeches, but Marlow makes reference to them, so they must have been uttered aloud. In these comments, the river is humanized, endowed with subjectivity, seen from a communal perspective. Spread out in "tranquil dignity," the "venerable stream" rests "unruffled . . . after ages of good service done to the race that peopled its banks." The men who have followed the sea look at it "not in the vivid flush of a short day that comes and departs forever, but in the august light of abiding memories." The "tidal current," which has run "to and fro in its unceasing service," is "crowded with memories of men and ships it had borne to the rest of home or to the battles of the sea." It has "known and served all the men of whom the nation is proud" and has "borne all the ships whose names are like jewels flashing in the night of time." The history of which the Thames is a part is a "gigantic tale." "Hunters for gold or pursuers of fame," the "great knights-errant of the sea" had all "gone out on that stream, bearing the sword, and often the torch, messengers of the might within the land, bearers of a spark from the sacred fire."

After his experience in the Congo, Marlow sees nature, civilization, and human history very differently than he did before; and these sentiments of his friends, with which he might once have concurred, seem ludicrous in the light of what he now knows. He does not laugh in their faces, but he cannot refrain from puncturing their illusions, as his were punctured in Africa. "And this also," he says suddenly, "has been one of the dark places of the earth". . . .

England Was Once Rome's Colony

Marlow's friends see the Thames as part of a thoroughly humanized world, as having a long and glorious history and being a servant of men's designs. Marlow sees it in terms of his Congo experience, which has thrown "a kind of light on everything about [him]—and into [his] thoughts." He communicates his vision by taking his auditors back to Roman times, when the Thames was a place of darkness. They see the Thames as the center of things, whence "greatness" floats "into the mystery of an unknown earth." However, for a Roman commander of a trireme ordered to Britain the Thames was "the very end of the world," much as the Congo was for Marlow:

> Sandbanks, marshes, forests, savages—precious little to eat fit for a civilized man, nothing but Thames water to drink. . . . Here and there a military camp lost in a wilderness, like a needle in a bundle of hay—cold, fog, tempests, disease, exile, and death—death skulking in the air, in the water, in the bush. They must have been dying like flies here.

Except for climate, the Thames then was much like the Congo now.

The experience of Marlow's Roman commander is similar to his own, as, up to a point, is that of his "decent young citizen in a toga," who feels "in some inland post" that "savagery," "utter savagery" has "closed round him—all that mysterious life of the wilderness that stirs in the forest, in the jungles, in the hearts of wild men. There is no initiation either into such mysteries. He has to live in the midst of the incomprehensible, which is also detestable." Marlow struggled in the Congo with the unintelligibility of his surroundings and was distressed at being driven out of his conception of the world. In some ways the decent young citizen resembles Kurtz more than Marlow. He is in Britain, as Kurtz is in the Congo, "to mend his fortunes." Once he is there, the mysterious life of the wilderness has "a fascination" that "goes to work upon him. The fascination of the abomination—you know, imagine the growing regrets, the longing to escape, the powerless disgust, the surrender, the hate." This is exactly what happens to Kurtz. Marlow, too, has been subject to the fascination of the abomination, although he has not surrendered to it. Before he goes to the Congo, he is fascinated by the shape of the river and, once there, by Kurtz. . . .

Marlow makes a distinction between conquerors and colonizers. The Romans, he says, "were no colonists; their administration was merely a squeeze. . . . They were conquerors, and for that you want only brute strength—nothing to boast of, when you have it, since your strength is just an accident arising from the weakness of others. They grabbed what they could get for the sake of what was to be got. It was just robbery with violence, and men going at it blind." Again, this parallels what Marlow saw going on in the Congo and prefigures the disdain he will express toward the predatory activities of the Europeans there. The "conquest of the earth, which mostly means the taking it away from those who have a different complexion or slightly flatter noses than ourselves, is not a pretty thing when you look into it too much"—and Marlow has looked into it closely in Africa. . . .

The Stated Intentions of Colonizers

For Marlow, the major difference between conquest and colonization is that conquerors are pursuing selfish objectives— wealth, fame, power, adventure—whereas colonists are out to establish a civilized order in which the welfare of the community is paramount. He himself goes to the Congo for adventure, in the pursuit of personal ends; but he is a different man when he returns. What redeems the conquest of the earth, he tells his listeners, is an "idea at the back of it; not a sentimental pretense but an idea; and an unselfish belief in the idea— something you can set up, and bow down before, and offer a sacrifice to."

The colonization of the Congo was undertaken in the name of the civilizing ideals espoused by the company, by the government of Belgium, and most eloquently by Kurtz; but the motive was exploitation, and the ideals were all "rot," "humbug," sentimental pretense. There was nothing unselfish about the enterprise. The Europeans were intent on sacrificing the natives to their greed rather than making any sacrifices themselves—though many paid for their rapacity with their lives. Marlow's Congo experience has thrown a kind of light on the conquest of other lands by technologically advanced Europeans, and he seems to be commenting indirectly on his companions' exaltation of the "dreams of men, the seed of commonwealths, the germs of empires" that had floated out on Thames. . . .

Marlow does not initially seem to be looking for empathy—this is something that emerges as he launches into his tale. At the outset he appears to be in the grip of a need to confront his companions' illusions. He had felt exasperated by the silly dreams of the inhabitants of Brussels, but these were people he did not know, or did not respect, or thought he should shield. With his friends on the *Nellie* he feels it is safe to speak his mind. They are men enough to be told what he has learned. He has an urge to display his superior knowledge and his ability to articulate it. . . .

The Colonizers' Charity Replaced by Egotism

In the Congo he sees where adventurism can lead, for both nations and individuals, with Kurtz being the most spectacular example. As a result, he becomes highly suspicious of the quest for wealth, power, and glory; and this is one of the reasons he reacts as he does to his companions' celebration of the men who had sailed out on the Thames. It is also one of the reasons he is so disturbed by his own fascination with Kurtz, for it indicates a kindred craving for personal glory that he needs to repudiate. He has come to see the danger of a hankering for exploration of the dark or unknown regions of the earth, or of the human heart, such as has motivated him.

The only thing that redeems the conquest of the earth is an unselfish belief in the idea at the back of it, "something you can set up, and bow down before, and offer a sacrifice to." The idea at the back of it must be that of subduing the forces inimical to order, both in our own natures and in the world around us, for the sake of the common good. But instead of serving something greater than himself, Kurtz seeks to become an object of veneration to whom others bow down and offer a sacrifice. Having begun as a romantic individualist, Marlow comes to preach the submersion of the self in the communal enterprise.

The Irony of Marlow's Narration Shows Him to Be a Semicolonialist

Anthony Fothergill

Anthony Fothergill has taught at Kenyon College, the University of Heidelberg, and the University of Exeter. He has widely published on Joseph Conrad.

The central question about Heart of Darkness *is what the novel reveals about Conrad's and Marlow's views of colonialism. The novel is not mythic but starkly realistic, based on accounts of King Leopold's policies and practices in the Congo that led to a decline of 6 million people in the population. His selection of details seems to make his own anticolonialism solid. But Marlow is an ironic narrator; that is, the reader knows more from Marlow's narration than Marlow does, and he does not reflect Conrad's view. He disapproves of colonialism merely because it is inefficient, yet he does recognize the connection between the efficient accountant and men dying in the grove. Marlow's account of Kurtz's brilliance is also in stark contrast to the end of Kurtz's report: "Exterminate all the brutes!" The contradictions that Marlow displays are not resolved, leaving reason to label him a "semicolonialist."*

Explosions and economics are a central configuration of the civilizing mission in Africa which *Heart of Darkness* records. A mythic reading of the novel ..., cannot, in my view, encompass this configuration: it 'mythologizes' historical realities. ...

Anthony Fothergill, "Colonialism; Semi-Colonialism," *Heart of Darkness*, Philadelphia: Open University Press, 1989, pp. 37–43, 47–49, 56–58. Reproduced by permission of the author.

Not Myth, but Reality

[It] dissolves into abstraction Conrad's experience of the specific form of colonial imperialism Leopold II practised in his Congo Free State for two decades from 1885. I am not using the term 'imperialism' as a mere swear-word. Rather, I mean the specific territorial conquests made by the industrialized European nations in their 'Scramble for Africa' in the second half of the nineteenth century. The historical causes and nature of this imperial expansion have been the subject of much critical debate. Suffice it to say that what was unusual about Leopold II's imperial presence in the Congo was that it became his personal territorial possession (rather than the Belgian State's). It was, in fact, recognized as such by the Berlin Conference of 1885, which arbitrated over European territorial ambitions in Africa, dividing the spoils primarily with the aim of averting conflict among the competing European nations. Moreover, Leopold pursued his Congo interests in the name of philanthropy and anti-slavery. As he himself stated:

> The mission which the agents of the State have to accomplish on the Congo is a noble one. They have to continue the development of civilization in the centre of Equatorial Africa, receiving their inspiration directly from Berlin and Brussels. Placed face to face with primitive barbarism, grappling with sanguinary customs that date back thousands of years, they are obliged to reduce these gradually. They must accustom the population to general laws, of which the most needful and the most salutary is assuredly that of work.

The ironies of such rhetoric were not lost on Conrad.

The Berlin Conference circumscribed Leopold's absolute personal rule over almost one million square miles of Africa by regulations which guaranteed free trade among European nations and companies there (and the forbidding of differential dues). . . . To exploit fully the wealth of the Congo State, he instituted a 'labour tax' on natives in the form of forty hours per month of forced labour. In practice this was brutally and arbitrarily exacted by the chiefs of the concession companies with the ruthless encouragement of Leopold's local army. Increased production of ivory and rubber was their only priority, physical mutilation and abuse their method. . . .

In effect, the Congo Free State was founded on the blood of a vast force of slave labour. Estimates for the 'decline' of the native population range from three to six million during the period of Leopold's personal tenancy. . . .

I cite this information partly to offer, however briefly, a historical context for the novel, but also as a way of contextualizing Kurtz and our reading of him. As so much depends on Marlow's (and our) interpretation of Kurtz, critics have not surprisingly devoted time to searching out models Conrad might have used. In their assiduous historical researches both Norman Sherry and Ian Watt have championed the candidature of some half-dozen possibles. With each new candidate, the aim of the undertaking itself, the search for a single model, is revealed to be more problematic. The very proliferation points to a new conclusion: that in his extreme monomania, brutality, and drive for self-aggrandizement, Kurtz is instancing what was an extreme but by no means unique expression of European civilization in its colonizing form. Marlow might be aghast at Kurtz's insane and tormented delusions:

> The wastes of his weary brain were haunted by shadowy images now—images of wealth and fame revolving obsequiously round his unextinguishable gift of noble and lofty expression. My Intended, my station, my career, my ideas— these were the subjects for the occasional utterances of elevated sentiments.

But Kurtz's discourse starts to look like a model of restrained modesty compared with Leopold's (presumably sane) declaration: 'The King was the founder of the State; he was its organizer, its owner, its absolute sovereign'. . . .

Conrad's View of King Leopold

[Conrad's] letters and the *Congo Diary* testify to the increasing sense of disillusionment and frustration and the severe physical and mental deterioration and collapse he suffered there. But they also suggest that his disenchantment was personal rather than political. Indeed, it may well be that he *saw* less evidence of brutality and mutilation than he was later to read about in the growing number of official reports and newspaper articles coming out of Central Africa on atrocities and exploitation. But though the sources for the novel's political critique were therefore not just personal experience, *Heart of Darkness* leaves little doubt about Conrad's verdict on Leopold's rule. It was unequivocal. In a letter to his publisher, Blackwood, of 31 December, 1898, outlining the idea of *(The) Heart of Darkness*, he talks of 'the criminality of inefficiency and pure selfishness when tackling the civilizing work in Africa', and in one of his last essays he remembers his Congo journey and night time by the Stanley Falls ('the Inner Station'):

> [T]here was no shadowy friend to stand by my side in the night of the enormous wilderness, no great haunting memory, but only the unholy recollection of a prosaic newspaper 'stunt' and the distasteful knowledge of the vilest scramble for loot that ever disfigured the history of human conscience and geographical exploration. What an end to the idealized realities of a boy's daydreams! . . .

Targeting All Colonialism

Military intervention here is seen primarily by Marlow as incomprehensible and absurd. Again, as with Fresleven, we find a discrepancy between cause and effect, purpose and achievement. How is this realized? A lot has to do with the recurrent emphasis on size and physical disproportion ('little', 'small flame would dart' juxtaposed against 'immensity', 'continent'). And the 'insanity' is made none the less an 'insanity' by its being a brutally regular occurrence ('The French had one of their wars going on thereabouts'), or by the explanation Marlow is offered, with its verbal mendacity to which he draws attention ('natives—he called them enemies!'). Incidentally, the fact that it is a *French* ship seems to widen Conrad's attack; it surely gives us grounds for concluding that his critique has a more general application to other (or all?) European colonial powers. . . .

Marlow's Independent Perspective

I think, in his perception of the French man-of-war we can see the positive aspect of his 'distance' from events. As observer and narrator he embraces the role of outsider: in his account, the deconstruction of the action into discrete entities is paralleled by an equivalent unpacking of the rhetoric of conquest. By putting the 'ordinary' occurrence of naval shelling under the microscope of detailed and alienated observation, Marlow 'de-familiarizes' it and releases himself (and the reader) from the unquestioning view of his fellow travellers on board, who would take a statement like 'The French are shelling enemy camps' for granted. His marginality permits a dual—and devastating—perspective. . . .

The victims of colonialism are not just the natives who are enslaved and the physical environment that is ravaged, but the victimizers, too, those who are the white instruments of empire-building. Like a destructive machine, once set in action it owes no more allegiance to its creator and agents than to its most obvious victims. Like the old knitters indifferent to Marlow's fate, the colonial machine doesn't particularly seem to care for anything but material gain. . . .

Conrad's Images of Brutality

Startling and brutal images demand notice. The chain-gang and the blacks dying in the grove of death greet Marlow as his first encounter with company 'methods'. Later the attack on his boat is so presented as to accentuate, through the tactic of delayed disclosure, the increasing sense of the bizarre and incomprehensible. Marlow sees the poleman 'inexplicably give up the business suddenly and stretch himself flat on the deck'; the gesture is dwelt on because it *appears* meaningless—then Marlow realizes they are under attack. The 'foolish' helmsman falls inexplicably at his feet; his feet get warm and wet—from the dying helmsman's blood. And surely most horrific of all is the double-sighting of the posts encircling Kurtz's house, seen first as ornamental carvings, eventually leaping into view as human skulls—graphic and symbolic testimony to Kurtz's lack of 'restraint'. These moments, possibly the most powerfully visualized in the novel, seem to me to share in stark brutality. . . .

Anticolonialist or Colonialist?

Still, the question has to be faced: how specifically *does* Conrad register these human subjects? Does he render them fully and concretely? In a forceful attack on Conrad as 'a bloody racist', the Nigerian novelist Chinua Achebe argues that Conrad is not really interested in Africa or Africans; he uses the country 'as a setting and backdrop which eliminates the African as a human factor . . . as a metaphysical battlefield devoid of all recognizable humanity, into which the wandering European enters at his peril'. . . .

I would agree that they are not personally characterized (in the way that the chief accountant, the fastidious pigeon-loving boiler-maker, the first-class agent are—though perhaps these portraits border on caricature). But in his depiction of his encounters with them, early on in his journey, we are surely given some sense of differentiation, of different histories, however fleeting. Some he recognizes as brutally displaced from their tribal homes: 'Brought from all the recesses of the coast in all the legality of time contracts, lost in uncongenial surroundings, fed on unfamiliar food, they sickened,

Statue of King Leopold II of Belgium, whose colonial government was responsible for the brutal deaths of millions of Congolese people, was re-erected in Kinshasa in 2005 to remind people of the horrors of Congo's colonial rule. © AP Images.

became inefficient, and were then allowed to crawl away and rest'. This, surely, casts the European stereotypes of 'inefficient' and 'listless' blacks in a new light. Later at the Central Station, there is a *suggestion* of Africans resisting their enslavement by an act of sabotage (burning the storehouse).

A further and telling portrait of detribalization can be found in the figure of the black overseer to the chain-gang. . . .

In the main, the traders, missionaries, and administrators who came to Central Africa did not even imagine 'imagining the other'. In this respect Marlow is different. When he is at his most equine, Marlow tries to imagine. This usually takes the form of acknowledging to himself that Africans pose a question, a mystery. . . .

For Marlow, the blacks pose questions potentially explicable within their own terms and norms. For example, Marlow is ready to *ask*, at least, whether the drums he hears in the distance don't have as normal a place in tribal culture, 'as profound a meaning as the sound of bells in a Christian country.' Similarly, he asks whether a deserted village would strike us as that odd if we translated the context to a Kentish village between Deal and Gravesend suddenly threatened by the invasion of 'a lot of mysterious niggers armed with all kinds of fearful weapons'. The startlingly incongruous white-worsted neckwear on one of the dying 'black shadows' provokes questions which ask for a history, but the questions do not get stereotypic answers involving superstition or fetishism—which other Europeans, who of course never wear crosses or lucky charms, might proffer.

In the specific instance of the black guard, Marlow 'imagines the other' this far: he silently acknowledges one of the stereotypic racist ways in which the 'superior' white man sees the black. . . .

The Irony of "Victims" and "Efficiency"

The written work itself, the actions it narrates, can provide a critical context within which we can assess Marlow's judgements. True, all the events of the tale are narrated by Marlow and filtered through the 'anonymous'. But Marlow is not creator of the (fictional) world he describes. Conrad can still organize the structure of and actions in that world in a way which can comment on Marlow's construing of it. The work will always say more than its narrator will or can explicitly tell. A discourse of actions can supply a critical viewpoint on Marlow's discourse of language. . . .

There may be no explicit qualification of the 'miracle of efficiency', but Marlow goes on immediately to record without comment the accountant's annoyance at the groans of an invalided agent which 'distract [his] attention'. The last view Marlow allows us of him is: 'turned to his work . . . bent over his books, [he] was making correct entries of perfectly correct transactions; and fifty feet below the doorstep I could see the still treetops of the grove of death'. There is a necessary political connection between the two clauses (or rather what they refer to). The semi-colon, a sign of the written text, not spoken narration, is a precise notation of Marlow's relation to both sides of the colonial coin: it insists upon a connection without dictating the precise nature of it. Standing in the doorway, Marlow mediates between the two faces of colonialism. He can see—and thus mediate to his audience—the link which the accountant cannot see, and which his statistics, dying in the grove, are perhaps beyond seeing now. It is a perfect physical figure to represent Marlow's own hovering between the administrator and the barbarity he perpetuates. Marlow's semi-colonialism, so to speak, does not fully resolve the contradictions of his position. . . .

Kurtz as the Epitome of Colonialism

Such narrative juxtapositions can be seen as Conrad's way of placing Marlow, and ironically commenting on his cult of efficiency. They also disclose to Marlow's listeners and Conrad's readers an important fact about Kurtz and how we should read *him*. He is not a unique perversion of the European civilizing mission; rather he can be seen as its epitome. Conrad insists upon Kurtz's cosmopolitan representativeness. 'All Europe contributed to the making of Kurtz' and he had all the benefits of Englishmen and Frenchmen among his forebears. To nurture his cultural values 'the original Kurtz had been educated partly in England, and . . . his sympathies were in the right place.' The upshot of this cultural heritage could hardly have been more chillingly recorded than in the scrawled footnote of Kurtz's report on the Suppression of Savage Customs. This 'beautiful piece of writing' concludes with the forthright injunction, 'Exterminate all the brutes!' It incorporates the same contradictions of the civilizing will as the miraculous chief accountant and his efficient book-keeping. Opposition to Kurtz within the Company comes because he's seen as a successful rival, not an immoral renegade; his development is the 'logical' extension, not the renunciation, of its practices. . . .

Marlow Is a Semicolonialist

To summarize . . . : I have tried to show how the work can and should be read within, and be seen to register, the historical realities of African colonization. Marlow's particular role is to offer a radical critique of these processes while at the same time revealing the contradictions in his own status. The primary *formal* techniques Conrad employs—of delayed revelation and ironic comment—carry their own benefits in the devastating criticism of the brutalities of colonization and how these actions are normally seen and represented. But they also carry disadvantages. The mystery of the subject sometimes seems like mystification. And the basis for the critique of colonial presence seems to resolve itself at times into the measure of efficiency. But the text finally rests with the displaying (not resolving) of contradictions—epitomized in Marlow's semi-colonialism.

Kurtz's Evil Is in Adopting Darkness

Patrick Brantlinger

Patrick Brantlinger, professor emeritus at Indiana University, is the author of several books on cultural history.

Whereas Marlow appears to condemn Belgium for its colonial policies in the Congo, he condones English imperialism. Joseph Conrad's style and his narrator make it difficult to discern his own view. Conrad's words in other documents condemn what European colonialism had become in the late nineteenth century, and he had friends who were anticolonialist, but he never engaged in anticolonialist causes. He had read about all the colonialists' beheadings, cannibalism, and amputations. His stance in the novel is difficult to pin down because of his impressionistic style. Although, finally, there is little question of the novel's anticolonialism, the reason seems to be because colonialists adopt blackness which Conrad identifies with evil. The conclusion to Conrad's stance on colonialism lies with Conrad's and Marlow's observations of Kurtz. Is he the epitome of corrupt imperialism, the evil of going native, or is he the hero who finally faces the horror?

[I]an] Watts is one of the many critics who interpret *Heart of Darkness* as an exposé of imperialist rapacity and violence. Kurtz's career in deviltry obviously undermines imperialist ideology, and the greed of the "faithless pilgrims"—the white sub-Kurtzes, so to speak—is perhaps worse. "The conquest of the earth," Marlow declares, "which mostly means the

Patrick Brantlinger, "Epilogue: Kurtz's 'Darkness' and Conrad's *Heart of Darkness*," *Criticism*, Wayne State University Press, 1988, pp. 256–264, 271–274. Reproduced by permission.

taking it away from those who have a different complexion or slightly flatter noses than ourselves, is not a pretty thing when you look into it too much." There is nothing equivocal about that remark; Conrad entertained no illusions about imperialist violence. But Marlow distinguishes between British imperialism and that of the other European powers: the red parts of the map are good to see, he says, "because one knows that some real work is done in there". *Heart of Darkness* is specifically about what Conrad saw in [Belgium's] King Leopold's African empire in 1890; it is unclear how far his critique can be generalized to imperialism beyond the Congo. . . .

Conrad's impressionism is for some critics his most praiseworthy quality; to others it appears instead a means of obfuscation, allowing him to mask his nihilism or to maintain contradictory values, or both. Interpretations of *Heart of Darkness* which read it as only racist (and therefore imperialist), or as only anti-imperialist (and therefore antiracist), inevitably founder on its impressionism. To point to only the most obvious difficulty, the narrative frame filters everything that is said not just through Marlow but also through the anonymous primary narrator. At what point is it safe to assume that Conrad/Marlow expresses a single point of view? And even supposing Marlow to speak directly for Conrad, does Conrad/Marlow agree with the values expressed by the primary narrator? Whatever our answers, *Heart of Darkness* offers a powerful critique of at least some manifestations of imperialism and racism as it simultaneously presents that critique in ways that can be characterized only as imperialist and racist. Impressionism is the fragile skein of discourse which expresses—or disguises—this schizophrenic contradiction as an apparently harmonious whole. Analysis of that contradiction helps to reveal the ideological constraints upon a critical understanding of imperialism in literature before World War I. It also suggests how imperialism influenced the often reactionary politics of literary modernism. . . .

Conrad's Statements About Imperialism

At least it is certain that Conrad was appalled by the "high-sounding rhetoric" used to mask the "sordid ambitions" of King Leopold II of Belgium, Conrad's ultimate employer during his six months in the Congo in 1890. *Heart of Darkness* expresses not only what Conrad saw and partially recorded in his "Congo Diary" but also the revelations of atrocities which began appearing in the British press as early as 1888 and reached a climax twenty years later, in 1908, when the mounting scandal forced the Belgian government to take control of Leopold's private domain. During that period the population of the Congo was decimated, perhaps halved; as many as six million persons may have been uprooted, tortured, and murdered through the forced labor system used to extract ivory and what reformers called "red rubber" from "the heart of darkness." Conrad was sympathetic toward the Congo Reform Association, established in 1903 partly by Roger Casement, whom he had met in Africa, and Casement got him to write a propaganda letter in which Conrad says: "It is an extraordinary thing that the conscience of Europe which seventy years ago . . . put down the slave trade on humanitarian grounds tolerates the Congo state today." There follows some patronizing language contrasting the brutalities visited upon the Congolese with the legal protections given to horses in Europe, but Conrad's intention is clear enough.

Congo Reform Association

There is little to add to Hunt Hawkins's account of Conrad's relations with the Congo Reform Association. The association's leader, Edmund Morel, who quoted Conrad's letter to Casement in *King Leopold's Rule in Africa* (1904), called *Heart of Darkness* the "most powerful thing ever written on the subject." But as Hawkins notes, apart from his letter to Casement, Conrad backed away from involvement with the association. Other prominent novelists who had never been to the Congo contributed as much or more to its work. Mark Twain volunteered "King Leopold's Soliloquy," and Arthur Conan Doyle wrote a book for the association called *The Crime of the Congo.* Conrad, as Hawkins notes, "had little faith in agitation for political reform because words were meaningless, human nature unimprovable, and the universe dying"—hardly views to encourage engagement in the cause of the association. . . .

What Conrad Learned After the Congo

Conrad did not base his critique of imperialist exploitation in *Heart of Darkness* solely on what he had seen in the Congo. What he witnessed was miserable enough, and personally he was also made miserable and resentful by disease and the conviction that his Belgian employers were exploiting him. As he assured Casement, however, while in the Congo he had not even heard of "the alleged custom of cutting off hands among the natives." The conclusion that Casement drew was that most of the cruelties practiced in the Congo were not traditional but the recent effects of exploitation. The cutting off of hands was a punishment for non-cooperation in Leopold's forced labor system and probably became frequent only after 1890. Moreover, just as Conrad had seen little or no evidence of torture, so he probably saw little or no evidence of cannibalism, despite the stress upon it in his story.

It thus seems likely that much of the horror either depicted or suggested in *Heart of Darkness* represents not what Conrad saw but rather his reading of the literature that exposed Leopold's bloody system between Conrad's return to England and his composition of the novella in 1898–99, along with many of the earlier works that shaped the myth of the Dark Continent. Although Conrad's "Congo Diary" and every facet of his journey to Stanley Falls and back have been scrutinized by Norman Sherry and others, what Conrad learned about the Congo after his sojourn there has received little attention. The exposé literature undoubtedly confirmed suspicions that Conrad formed in 1890, but the bloodiest period in the history of Leopold's regime began about a year later. According to Edmund Morel: "From 1890 onwards the records of the Congo State have been literally blood-soaked. Even at that early date, the real complexion of Congo State philanthropy was beginning to appear, but public opinion in Europe was then in its hoodwinked stage."

Conrad's Sources

The two events that did most to bring Leopold's Congo under public scrutiny were the 1891–94 war between Leopold's forces and the Arab slave-traders and the execution of Charles Stokes, British citizen and renegade missionary, by Belgian officers in 1895. The conflict with the Arabs—a "war of extermination," according to Morel—was incredibly cruel and bloody. "The first serious collision with the Arabs occurred in October 27, 1891; the second on May 6, 1892. Battle then succeeded battle; Nyangwe, the Arab stronghold, was captured in January, 1893, and with the surrender of Rumaliza in January, 1894, the campaign came to an end." Conrad undoubtedly read about these events in the press and perhaps also in later accounts, notably Captain Sidney Hinde's *The Fall of the Congo Arabs* (1897). Arthur Hodister, whom Sherry claims as the original of Kurtz, was an early victim of the fighting, having led an expedition to Katanga which was crushed by the Arabs. According to Ian Watt, "*The Times* reported of Hodister and his comrades that 'their heads were stuck on poles and their bodies eaten.'" This and many similar episodes during the war are probable sources for Conrad's emphasis upon cannibalism in *Heart of Darkness*.

Cannibalism was practiced by both sides, not just the Arabs and their Congolese soldiers. According to Hinde, who must also be counted among possible models for Kurtz, "the fact that both sides were cannibals, or rather that both sides had cannibals in their train, proved a great element in our success." Muslims, Hinde points out, believe they will go to heaven only if their bodies are intact. So cannibalism was a weapon of fear and reprisal on both sides, as well as a traditional accompaniment of war among some Congolese societies. Hinde speaks of combatants on both sides as "human wolves" and describes numerous "disgusting banquets." A typical passage reads: "What struck me most in these expeditions was the number of partially cut-up bodies I found in every direction for miles around. Some were minus the hands and feet, and some with steaks cut from the thighs or elsewhere; others had the entrails or the head removed, according to the taste of the individual savage." Hinde's descriptions of such atrocities seem to be those of an impartial, external observer, but in fact he was one of six white officers in charge of some four hundred "regulars" and about twenty-five thousand "cannibal" troops. His expressions of horror are what one expects of an Englishman; they are also those of a participant, however, and contradict his evident fascination with every bloodthirsty detail.

Colonial Heinousness and Slavery

It seems likely that Conrad read Hinde's lurid account. He must have known about the war also from earlier accounts, such as those in the *Times,* and from E.J. Glave's documenting of "cruelty in the Congo Free State" for the *Century Magazine* in 1896–97. According to Glave, "the state has not suppressed slavery, but established a monopoly by driving out the Arab and Wangwana competitors." Instead of a noble war to end the slave trade, which is how Leopold and his agents justified their actions against the Arabs, a new system of slavery was installed in place of the old. Glave continues: "Sometimes the natives are so persecuted that they [take revenge] by killing and eating their tormentors. Recently the state post on the Lomami lost two men killed and eaten by the natives. Arabs were sent to punish the natives; many women and children were taken, and twenty-one heads were brought to [Stanley Falls], and have been used by Captain Rom as a decoration round a flower-bed in front of his house." Captain Rom, no doubt, must also be counted among Kurtz's forebears. In any event, the practice of seizing Congolese for laborers and chopping off the hands and heads of resisters continued, probably increasing after the defeat of the Arabs, as numerous eyewitnesses testify in the grisly quotations that form the bulk of Morel's exposés. According to a typical account by a Swiss observer: "If the chief does not bring the stipulated number of baskets [of raw rubber], soldiers are sent out, and the people are killed without mercy. As proof, parts of the body are brought to the factory. How often have I watched heads and hands being carried into the factory." . . .

The Evil of "Going Native"

One difficulty . . . is that Conrad portrays the moral bankruptcy of imperialism by showing European motives and actions as no better than African fetishism and savagery. He paints Kurtz and Africa with the same tar-brush. His version of evil—the form taken by Kurtz's Satanic behavior—is going native. Evil, in short, *is* African in Conrad's story; if it is also European, that is because some white men in the heart of darkness behave like Africans. Conrad's stress on cannibalism, his identification of African customs with violence, lust, and madness, his metaphors of bestiality, death, and darkness, his suggestion that traveling in Africa is like traveling backward in time to primeval, infantile, but also hellish stages of existence—these features of the story are drawn from the repertoire of Victorian imperialism and racism that painted an entire continent dark. . . .

Ambiguity About Colonialism

Conrad knows that his story is ambiguous: he stresses that ambiguity at every opportunity, so that labeling the novella anti-imperialist is as unsatisfactory as condemning it for being

Two enslaved Congolese men in manacles and chains, circa 1904. Under King Leopold II's colonial regime, natives were forced to work in chain gangs. © Universal Images Group/ Hulton Archive/Getty Images.

racist. The fault-line for all of the contradictions in the text lies between Marlow and Kurtz and, of course, it also lies between Conrad and both of his ambiguous characters (not to mention the anonymous primary narrator). Is Marlow Kurtz's antagonist, critic, and potential redeemer? Or is he Kurtz's pale shadow and admirer, his double, finally one more idolator in a story full of fetishists and devil worship? Conrad poses these questions with great care, but he just as carefully refrains from answering them. . . .

Kurtz and Conrad's Hollow Voices

Kurtz's devious, shadowy voice echoes Conrad's. It is just this hollow voice, eloquently egotistical, capable both of high idealism and of lying propaganda, which speaks from the center of the heart of darkness to sum up and to judge.

Besides being a painter, musician, orator, and universal genius, Kurtz is also, like Conrad, a writer. What he writes is both an analogue for the story and its dead center, the kernel of meaning or nonmeaning within its cracked shell. True, Kurtz has not written much, only seventeen pages, but "it was a beautiful piece of writing." His pamphlet for the International Society for the Suppression of Savage Customs is a summa of imperialist rhetoric, which Marlow describes as "eloquent, vibrating with eloquence, but too high-strung, I think":

> He began with the argument that we whites, from the point of development we had arrived at, "must necessarily appear to [savages] in the nature of supernatural beings—we approach them with the might as of a deity," and so on, and so on. "By the simple exercise of our will we can exert a power for good practically unbounded," etc., etc. From that point he soared and took me with him. The peroration was magnificent, though difficult to remember, you know. It gave me the notion of an exotic Immensity ruled by an august Benevolence. It made me tingle with enthusiasm. This was the unbounded power of eloquence [i.e., the unbounded will-to-style]. There were no practical hints to interrupt the magic current of phrases, unless a kind of note at the foot of the last page, scrawled evidently much later, in an un-

steady hand, may be regarded as the exposition of a method. It was very simple, and at the end of that moving appeal to every altruistic sentiment it blazed at you, luminous and terrifying, like a flash of lightning in a serene sky: "Exterminate all the brutes!"

Viewed one way, Conrad's anti-imperialist story clearly condemns Kurtz's murderous, imperialist categorical imperative. Viewed another way, Conrad's racist story voices that very imperative, and Conrad knows it. At the hollow center of *Heart of Darkness*, far from the misty halos and moonshine where the meaning supposedly resides, Conrad inscribes a text that, like the novel itself, cancels out its own best intentions. . . .

A Critique of Colonialism's Hypocrisy and Corruption

Kurtz's pamphlet, as well as what Marlow reveals about his unspeakable rites, allow us to understand his dying words as something more than an outcry of guilt and certainly more than a mere expression of the fear of death or of loathing for African savagery. Those words can be seen as referring to a lying idealism that can rationalize any behavior, to a complete separation between words and meaning, theory and practice. On this level, *Heart of Darkness* offers a devastating critique of imperialist ideology. . . .

Conrad's critique or empire is never strictly anti-imperialist. Instead, in terms that can be construed as both conservative and nihilistic, he mourns the loss of the true faith in modern times, the closing down of frontiers, the narrowing of the possibilities for adventure, the commercialization of the world and of art, the death of chivalry and honor. Here the meaning of his emphasis on the lying propaganda of modern imperialism becomes evident. What was once a true, grand, noble, albeit violent enterprise is now a "a gigantic and atrocious fraud"—except maybe, Marlow thinks, in the red parts of the map, where "some real work is done."

Heart of Darkness
Reveals Conrad's Ambivalence
Toward Colonialism

Frances B. Singh

A professor of English at Hostos Community College of the City University of New York, Frances B. Singh has published on colonialism in India, E.M. Forster, and Joseph Conrad.

As a youth, Conrad was a victim of Russian colonialism, and his decision to be a sailor was something of an escape from eastern Europe. But his profession would expose him to other colonized areas, particularly the Congo. Marlow, his narrator, attacks colonialism in three ways: by comparing it with the Roman sacking of England, by sarcastically exploring the invasion, and by condemning the exploitation with metaphors. However, Marlow's comments show that he believes that Africans corrupt the Europeans, and as a result, Marlow is not free of the colonial mentality. He sees Kurtz as depraved because of his attempt to embrace tribalism. If Marlow reflects Conrad's view of colonialism, then it is decidedly ambivalent in that he has sympathy with the victims of colonization but distrusts their ability to achieve civilization for themselves.

It is a truth universally acknowledged that *Heart of Darkness* is one of the most powerful indictments of colonialism ever written. Why this is so can be explained by reference to Conrad's own life. As a child Conrad was a victim of Russia's colonialistic policies toward Poland. On account of his father's revolutionary activities on behalf of Polish freedom, he, his mother, and his father were exiled to Siberia. When Conrad

Frances B. Singh, "The Colonial Bias of *Heart of Darkness*," *Conradiana*, vol. 10, 1978, pp. 41–42, 44–45, 49–52. Reproduced by permission of Texas Tech University Press.

grew up he chose to follow the sea as a career because he felt it would provide him with the sense of openness, freedom, and democracy he had not been able to feel in his childhood. Ironically the profession which he thought would take him away from the horror of colonialism often brought him closer to it.

Conrad's Congo Experience

Heart of Darkness grows out of one of Conrad's brushes with colonialism. In 1890 Conrad was given command of a river steamer plying among the trading stations set up by the Belgians along the Congo River. At that time the Belgian Congo was the most ruthlessly exploited region in the whole African continent, and what made the exploitation worse was that it went on under the cover of brotherhood and philanthropy. Conrad's experiences there form the basis of *Heart of Darkness*. In 1902 he said that its story was "mainly a vehicle for conveying a batch of personal impressions," and in the "Author's Note" to *Youth and Two Other Stories*, he described it as "experience pushed a little (and only very little) beyond the actual facts of the case." However Conrad does not tell the story directly; it is narrated by a character called Marlow.

Romans in England; Hypocrisy in Africa

Marlow's impressions of colonialism fall into three classes. The first type is a direct, straightforward attack and is exemplified in his descriptive analysis of the Roman colonization of ancient Britain:

> "They grabbed what they could get for the sake of what was to be got. It was just robbery with violence, aggravated murder on a great scale, and men going at it blind. . . . The conquest of the earth, which mostly means the taking it away from those who have a different complexion or slightly flatter noses than ourselves, is not a pretty thing when you look into it too much."

The second is ironic and is well illustrated by his references to the "noble cause," the "jolly pioneers of progress" and the "improved specimen" who was his fireman. His tone is also ironic as he comments on Kurtz's report for the International Society for the Suppression of Savage Customs: "'The peroration was magnificent, though difficult to remember, you know. It gave me the notion of an exotic Immensity ruled by an august Benevolence'" (p. 118). Marlow combines the attack direct with the attack through irony in his description of the Eldorado Exploring Expedition to heighten the immorality of its intentions:

> "This devoted band called itself the Eldorado Exploring Expedition, and I believe they were sworn to secrecy. Their talk, however, was the talk of sordid buccaneers: it was reckless without hardihood, greedy without audacity, and cruel without courage; there was not an atom of foresight or of serious intention in the whole batch of them, and they did not seem aware these things are wanted for the work of the world. To tear treasure out of the bowels of the land was their desire, with no more moral purpose at the back of it than there is in burglars breaking into a safe. Who paid the expenses of the noble enterprise I don't know. . . . "

Attacking Imperialism Through Language

The third and most important type of comment uses metaphor to lash out against colonialism. Thus Brussels is likened to a "whited sepulchre," and the offices of the trading company which runs the steamers on the Congo to "a house in a city of the dead." The African natives, victims of Belgian exploitation, are described as "shapes," "shadows" and "bundles of acute angles," so as to show the dehumanizing effect of colonialistic rule on the ruled. Kurtz becomes "an animated image of death carved out of old ivory," a "voice" and a "shadow," suggesting the loss of personality that colonialism effects on the rulers.

Of all the suggestive metaphors used in the story, however, there is nothing like the title itself. On one level it indicates merely the geographical location of the Belgian Congo and the color of its inhabitants. On another it refers to the evil practices of the colonizers of the Congo, their sordid exploitation of the natives, and suggests that the real darkness is not in Africa but in Europe, and that its heart is not in the breasts of black Africans but in all whites who countenance and engage in colonialistic enterprise. While on the first level the metaphor has a direct, factual, and straightforward application, on the second it is ironic, for what is apparently black is really white, and what is apparently white is really black. These two levels, therefore, correspond structurally to the first two classes into which Marlow's observations on colonialism fall. What unites these two interpretations of the metaphor is the fact that they are both based on real phenomena: the ethnography of the Congo, the nature and consequence of empire-building. . . .

Sympathy with Blacks Couched in Racism

Historically Marlow would have us feel that the Africans are the innocent victims of the white man's heart of darkness; psychologically and metaphysically he would have us believe that they have the power to turn the white man's heart black. That is, Marlow equates the primitive with the evil and physical blackness of Africans with a spiritual darkness. The physical is confused with the metaphysical, the literal with the metaphorical. But one cannot have it both ways. Marlow's feeling that Kurtz became depraved by turning to "the forest, to the bush, towards the gleam of fires, the throb of drums, the drone of weird incantations" as another man may catch a cold from getting caught in a storm is just a kind of transference of moral responsibility. Africa and Africans are his scapegoat for the existence of the powers of darkness in the white man and through him the heart of darkness which was first associated with the West gets reassociated with Africa.

Specifically Marlow believes Kurtz to have "taken a high seat amongst the devils of the land" because of his participation in certain tribal ceremonies which seem to have involved human sacrifice, cannibalism, and head-hunting. . . . His refusal to try to understand the significance of the rites of the Africans stems from his conviction that what he will be told will support his feeling that they are abominations. But by believing that these actual rites, the customs of the same people whom the Belgians were exploiting, are exercises in evil and that knowledge of them should be suppressed, Marlow is, in effect, a member of that colonialistic front for which Kurtz wrote, the International Society for the Suppression of Savage Customs. And as long as he refuses to understand their true significance, as long as he finds them to be a living example of the depths to which man can sink, as long as he believes they should be suppressed, then he has cried, along with every colonizer before and since, "Exterminate all the brutes."

Thus Marlow's sympathy for the oppressed blacks is only superficial. He feels sorry for them when he sees them dying, but when he sees them healthy, practising their customs, he feels nothing but abhorrence and loathing, like a good colonizer to whom such a feeling offers a perfect rationalization for his policies. If blacks are evil then they must be conquered and put under white man's rule for their own good. Marlow is trying to have it both ways, anti-colonialistic and anti-depravity, but as long as he associates the life of depravity with the life of blacks then he can hardly be called anti-colonial. He may sympathize with the plight of blacks, he may be disgusted by the effects of economic colonialism, but because he has no desire to understand or appreciate people of any culture other than his own, he is not emancipated from the mentality of a colonizer. . . .

Evil in Kurtz's Tribalism

Marlow reaches Kurtz and sides with him as the lesser of two evils because Kurtz recognizes his own depravity on his death-bed. Of what, however, did that depravity consist? According to Marlow Kurtz's depravity consisted of a terrible egotism which made him seek gratification for various lusts in "unlaw-ful" ways. These "unlawful" ways, however, seem to be nothing more than Kurtz's adoption of the customs of an African tribe. So what Marlow implies is that Kurtz's tribalization is a symbol of his depravity. From the little we see of Kurtz's fol-lowers, though, there is nothing to suggest that they are de-praved. Rather they appear as protective, simple and unself-conscious—far better specimens of humanity than the white people of *Heart of Darkness.* . . .

Kurtz's last words are "'The horror! The horror!'" and for Marlow the horror being referred to is the blackness of Kurtz's soul. But there is more to this blackness than meets Marlow's eye. I have just argued that Kurtz's depravity consisted not in giving in too much to the tribal way of life but in not giving in enough. If that is the case I would suggest that contrary to Marlow's implication the "horror" refers first to what Kurtz has done to the blacks and only secondarily to what he has done to himself, since the latter is only the effect, and not the cause of the former. Consequently the full application of Kurtz's last words would not only be to himself but also to men like Marlow who seemed to hate colonialism but really lived by its values and associated the practices of the blacks with the road to perdition.

"Brutes" May Refer to Colonizers

The other famous line in the story, "Exterminate all the brutes," is capable of a similar extended interpretation. Mar-low takes the word "brutes" to refer to the Africans and inter-prets the fact that the sentence comes at the end of a docu-ment written to suggest a better way of approaching the less

HOW THE ROMANS CAME TO BRITAIN.

THE LANDING OF THE ROMANS.

Frances B. Singh points out that in Heart of Darkness, *Marlow attacks colonialism by comparing it with the Roman invasion of Britain, depicted here.* © 2d Alan King/Alamy.

developed as meaning that Kurtz became more savage than the so-called savages. But Marlow's interpretation is tinged by a colonialistic bias. Given that Kurtz became one with an African tribe and learned to understand the meaning of their customs, his words may be taken to mean that the only way Africa could develop would be if the real brutes or savages, the colonizers, were removed. What Kurtz developed in the jungle, therefore, was not an "unlawful soul," but historical foresight.

115

To what extent, though, are Marlow's attitudes Conrad's? If it can be established that Conrad had different attitudes from Marlow on colonialism and evil, then *Heart of Darkness* would be Conrad's *Modest Proposal* [a satirical essay by Jonathan Swift], in that the author would be arguing something different from what his persona was preaching. Furthermore by showing Marlow's terms as limited, Conrad would be making the larger point that those who see others as less than human are themselves dehumanized by their own vision. On the other hand if Conrad shares Marlow's prejudices then *Heart of Darkness* was written, consciously or unconsciously, from a colonialistic point of view. . . .

At first glance it also looks as if the narrator who frames Marlow's story represents a more comprehensive point of view than Marlow, for his role is to interpret the meaning of the tale and give it a universal significance. However, the meaning he draws from it is ultimately no different from Marlow's. At the beginning of *Heart of Darkness*, he is an upholder of English colonialism, calling the English "bearers of a spark from the sacred fire." At the end he realizes that the Thames [River] leads "into the heart of an immense darkness," meaning that English colonizers are as evil as any other, and that those who set forth on colonialistic enterprises, no matter how nobly they were conceived, lose themselves in the process. Thus it would seem that the narrator, unlike Marlow, is a true critic of colonialism. . . .

Conrad's and Marlow's Ambivalence

On colonialism too Marlow projects Conrad's ideas. In 1899 Conrad wrote about the Boer War in a letter to a cousin: "That they—the Boers—are struggling in good faith for their independence cannot be doubted; but it is also a fact that they have no idea of liberty, which can only be found under the English flag all over the world." That is, Conrad sympathized with the Boers' struggle for independence, but he also believed that they were not capable of achieving much on their own. This ambivalent attitude toward the Boers is reflected in Marlow's attitude toward the blacks. He sympathizes with their plight when he stumbles into the grove of death, but finds nothing of value in their culture of "unspeakable rites," "satanic" litanies and "fiendish" rows.

Ambivalent, in fact, is probably the most accurate way to sum up Conrad's attitude toward colonialism. In 1899 he wrote both that "England alone sends out men ... with ... a transparent sincerity of feeling" and that "intentions will, no doubt count for something [i.e. when colonizing nations have to face the Day of Judgment], though, of course, every nation's conquests are paved with good intentions." He could talk ironically of [Rudyard] Kipling's accounts in a newspaper which "spoke much of the rights and duties of civilization, of the sacredness of the civilizing work, and extolled the merits of those who went about bringing light and faith and commerce to the dark places of the earth," but he could also write in a different key, as in his letter to *Blackwood's Magazine*: "The title I am thinking of is '*The Heart of Darkness*' but the narrative is not gloomy. The criminality of inefficiency and pure selfishness when tackling the civilizing work in Africa is a justifiable idea." But if a work is to be called truly anti-colonial then such ambivalence is not permissible, for it compromises the position. The compromises that Marlow makes, as when he fights off identification with the blacks or when he tells lies about Kurtz to prevent the civilized Western world from collapsing, stem from Conrad's own inability to face un-flinchingly the nature of colonialism. . . .

It seems to me that although Conrad was to some extent aware of some of the limitations of Marlow's attitudes and pointed them up in the story, he was not sensitive to all of them. In fact he transferred the most important ones to Mar-low, who therefore becomes his mouthpiece in the story for them.

Nevertheless although I have argued in this essay that Marlow's ethnocentricity leads him to side with the colonizers against the Africans and that this approach is shared by Conrad as well, I do not wish to suggest that Conrad intended *Heart of Darkness* as a vindication of colonialistic policies or that the story should be removed from the canon of works indicting colonialism. Rather my aim has been to illuminate the problem he ran into when he attempted to indict colonialism.

An African Defends Conrad's Anticolonialism

C.P. Sarvan

C.P. Sarvan of the University of Zambia is known for his refutation of Chinua Achebe's thesis on Joseph Conrad. He has published on French colonialism, Olive Schreiner, and Ferdinand Oyono.

African readers of Heart of Darkness *have differed widely in their views of Conrad and colonialism, but the seminal work attacking Conrad as a racist and imperialist was by Nigerian novelist Chinua Achebe. Sarvan argues that Conrad and Marlow are not one and the same; therefore, much of what Marlow says is not shared by Conrad. Conrad's focus is not on Africa and African character but on European colonial degeneracy. The "hair dresser's dummy," for example, is part of the "colonial machinery" that is inhuman and inhumane. The appearance of the colonialists is very different from their savage hearts. Conrad's powerful denunciation of colonialism has often been undervalued because of the failure to recognize Marlow as an ironic narrator, not the voice of Conrad who, though part of the imperialist age, is ahead of his time in condemning it.*

Conrad's setting, themes, and his triumph in writing major literature in his third language, have won him a special admiration in the non-European world. "The African writer and Joseph Conrad share the same world and that is why Conrad's world is so familiar. Both have lived in a world dominated by capitalism, imperialism, colonialism" [Ngugi Wa Thiong'o stated]. But African readers are also checked by, and disconcerted at, works such as *The Nigger of the "Narcissus"* and *Heart of Darkness*. The case against the latter was most strongly made by Chinua Achebe. . . .

C.P. Sarvan, "Racism and the *Heart of Darkness*," *The International Fiction Review*, vol. 7, no. 1, 1980, pp. 6–10. Reproduced by permission.

Achebe's Argument Against Conrad

Africa is "the other world," "the antithesis of Europe and therefore of civilization, a place where man's vaunted intelligence and refinement are finally mocked by triumphant bestiality." Achebe commented on Conrad's comparison of the Congo and the Thames [Rivers], and also alleged that the contrast made between the two women who loved Kurtz, one African, the other European, is highly prejudiced. Any sympathy expressed for the sufferings of the black African under colonialism, argued Achebe is a sympathy born of a kind of liberalism which whilst acknowledging distant kinship, repudiates equality. . . .

Marlow Is Not Conrad

I shall in the following pages attempt to narrowly limit myself to an examination of the charge of racism brought against Conrad's *Heart of Darkness.* Let us begin with the fictional Marlow whose story was once heard and is now related by a fictional narrator. "It might be contended . . . that the attitude to the African . . . is not Conrad's but that of his fictional narrator, Marlow. . . . [But] Marlow seems to me to enjoy Conrad's complete confidence." Marlow's portrait is drawn with quiet irony and, at times, a mocking humor which denotes "distance" between creator and character. For example, he is described as resembling an idol and he sits like a European Buddha without the lotus. Marlow claims to be deeply, almost pathologically averse to telling lies but we find that he prevaricates at least twice within this tale. He condemns the Roman conquest and contrasts it with the "superior" European colonialism:

> What saves us is efficiency—the devotion to efficiency. But these chaps were not much account, really. They were no colonists; their administration was merely a squeeze. . . . They were conquerors, and for that you only want brute force—nothing to boast of, when you have it, since your

strength is just an accident arising from the weakness of others. They grabbed what they could. . . . It was just robbery with violence, aggravated murder on a large scale. . . . The conquest of the earth, which mostly means the taking it away from those who have a different complexion or slightly flatter noses than ourselves, is not a pretty thing when you look into it too much. What redeems it is the idea only. An idea at the back of it; not a sentimental pretence but an idea; and unselfish belief in the idea.

A long quotation but necessary in that it again separates author from character. Significantly, this "idea" is presented in ambiguous "pagan" terms as "something you can set up, and bow down before, and offer a sacrifice to." What is more, the rest of the story shows that the European colonial conquest contrary to Marlow's claims, was much worse than that of the Romans. . . . Thus it is not correct to say that Marlow has Conrad's complete confidence, and even more incorrect to say that Conrad believed Europe to be in a state of grace. The glorious sailors proudly cited by Marlow were pirates and plunderers. This ironic distance between Marlow and Conrad should not be overlooked though the narrative method makes it all too easy. Nor can Conrad's very forceful criticisms of colonialism be lightly passed over as weak liberalism. What ships unload in Africa are soldiers and customhouse clerks: the one to conquer and the other to administer and efficiently exploit. The cannon pounds a continent and "the merry dance of death and trade goes on." This "rapacious and pitiless folly" attempts to pass itself off as philanthropy, and to hypocritically hide its true nature under words such as enemies, criminals, and rebels. The counterparts of enemies, criminals, and rebels are the emissaries of light, such as Kurtz! . . .

Darkness Is Colonialism, Not Africa

When the Romans looked down upon the people of Britain, and the Europeans upon "natives," it was because they felt they had achieved a much higher civilization than the people they were confronting and conquering. The contempt was not on grounds of race itself, and Conrad suggests that Europe's claim to be civilized and therefore superior, needs earnest re-examination. The reference in *Heart of Darkness* is not to a place (Africa), but to the condition of European man; not to a black people, but to colonialism. The crucial question is whether European "barbarism" is merely a thing of the historical past. Surely the contrast between savage African and "civilized" European, in the light of that greedy and inhuman colonialism, is shown to be "appearance" rather than reality. The emphasis, the present writer would suggest, is on continuity, on persistence through time and peoples, and therefore on the fundamental oneness of man and his nature. If a judgment has to be made, then uncomplicated "savagery" is better than the "subtle horrors" manifested by almost all the Europeans Marlow met on that ironic voyage of discovery. When Marlow speaks of the African in European service as one of the "reclaimed," it is grim irony for he has been reclaimed to a worse state of barbarism. Left to itself, Africa has a "greatness" that went "home to one's very heart." As Marlow begins his story, the light changes as though "stricken to death by the touch of that gloom brooding over a crowd of men": yet the gloom is very much over the Thames as well. The Thames as "a waterway leading to the uttermost ends of the earth" is connected with and therefore a part of those uttermost ends. The river signifies what is abiding in nature, in man, and in the nature of man, even as "the sea is always the same" and foreign shores and foreign faces are veiled not by mystery but by ignorance.

Insensitivity and Heartlessness

The immaculately dressed, fastidious, and sensitive hairdresser's dummy, a representative of civilized Europe and a part of the colonial machinery, is totally insensitive to the suffering he helps to cause and by which he is surrounded. (His extreme cleanliness is perhaps to be seen as compulsive, an attempt to keep clean in the midst of that moral dirt.) Even in the case of Kurtz, one must remember that all Europe had "contributed" to his making. As for pagan rites and savage dances, the Europeans with "imbecile rapacity" were "praying" to ivory, that is, to materialism, and one red-haired man "positively danced," bloodthirsty at the thought that he and the others "must have made a glorious slaughter" of the Africans in the bush. The alleged primitiveness of the boilerman only serves to show the similarity between his *appearance* and the *actions* of the "civilized." . . .

An Indictment of Colonialism

In a conversation with me, Ngugi Wa Thiong'o accepted some of Achebe's criticisms but felt he had overlooked the positive aspect, namely, Conrad's attack on colonialism. The skulls stuck on poles outside Kurtz's house, Wa Thiong'o said, was the most powerful indictment of colonialism. No African writer, he continued, had created so ironic, apt, and powerful an image: ironic when one considers that Kurtz and many others like him had come to "civilize" the non-European world; apt when one recalls what they really did. But Wa Thiong'o also observed that though Conrad (having experienced the evils of Czarist imperialism) castigates Belgian atrocities, he is much milder in his criticisms of British imperialism. This ambivalence, concluded Professor Wa Thiong'o, compromised Conrad's otherwise admirable stand. Leonard Kibera (Kenyan novelist, short story writer, critic, and teacher) wrote informally to me as follows: "I study *Heart of Darkness* as an examination of the West itself and not as a comment on Africa. Many Africans do get turned off Conrad because they feel he used the third world so totally as a background against which he examined Western values and conduct that the people in Africa and Asia are no more than caricatures. I do not object to this and appreciate the fact that in Conrad there is not that ... pretension of understanding the third world." Nadine Gordimer writing on another famous European in Africa states that [missionary David] Livingstone, reassessed, emerges as a fallible human being. Conrad too was not entirely immune to the infection of the beliefs and attitudes of his age, but he was ahead of most in trying to break free.

Social Issues
in Literature

CHAPTER 3

Contemporary
Perspectives
on Colonialism

A Poor Continent Rich in Resources

John Mukum Mbaku

John Mukum Mbaku is a professor of economics at Weber State University in Utah. He is the author of several books, including Corruption: Causes, Consequences, and Cleanups.

The problems of poverty and deprivation still plague Africa and Africans even though Africa is rich in natural resources. This is largely attributable to the devastating exploitation of the continent by their own corrupt governments which aid foreign companies and countries—in short, what is now called neocolonialism. Most of the continent's production of goods and harvesting of resources is for export to more powerful foreign economies. The government is able to seize land owned by farmers and turn it over to outside corporations. Transnational companies invited to "develop" African countries actually displace the people by taking away rights to their land, building dams that flood their land, and taking away their livelihoods. The situation is scarcely different from nineteenth-century colonization, especially in that the people have no voice in how their country is run. The environmental impact is also negative; for example, rain forests are decimated.

As the first decade of the new millennium continues to unfold, Africa and Africans continue to face many serious problems. Among these are extremely high levels of poverty and deprivation, especially among rural communities; the absence of governance structures that adequately constrain the exercise of government agency and the ability of politicians

John Mukum Mbaku, "The Environment and the New Globalization in Africa," *Africa and the New Globalization*, edited by George Klay Kieh Jr., Burlington, VT: Ashgate Publishing Co., 2008, pp. 129, 132–133, 139–140, 142, 151. Reproduced by permission of Ashgate Publishing Co.

and civil servants to engage in such opportunistic behaviors as corruption and rent seeking; the existence of resource allocation systems that stunt indigenous entrepreneurship and the creation of the wealth that Africans need to confront massive and pervasive poverty; and excessive exploitation of the continent's environmental resources and, agro-ecological degradation. Recent events in the Niger Delta region of Nigeria have forced the world to take a serious look at ecological degradation and its consequences on the African peoples.

Matters Contributing to Colonialism

However, it is important to emphasize that overexploitation of natural resources and environmental degradation—especially for the production of goods for export to the industrial market economies—is a continent-wide problem. As will be made evident in this chapter, the present patterns for the exploitation of Africa's natural resources and damage to its environment were set during the colonial period. First, we shall examine how patterns of resource exploitation that were established by European mercantile companies, with the help of the colonial state apparatus, have remained to this day. Second, we shall show that the overexploitation of the continent's environmental resources, primarily for the benefit of the metropolitan economies, has resulted in significant damage to Africa's environment. Increased globalization, which has been going on since the partition of the continent in the late 19th century, has produced trade patterns that have continued to impose severe damage on Africa's already fragile ecosystem. Third, we argue that poorly defined and unenforceable property rights in environmental resources—a consequence of the continent's inability to provide itself with locally-focused, relevant, and viable institutional arrangements—have been the main determinant of overexploitation and abuse, all of which have contributed not only to increased poverty in the continent, but have significantly endangered sustainability in the allocation of natural resources....

Unenforced Property Rights

At independence, most Africans believed that the new dispensation would change colonial trade patterns and enhance the ability of Africans to participate in global trade. However, most of the new leaders chose to retain the trade patterns inherited from the colonial state, allowing their countries to remain essentially suppliers of raw materials to the metropolitan economies and markets for the sale of excess output from the factories of their former colonizers. Although such economic dependency is a serious problem in Africa today, it is not a main concern of this [essay]. In this [essay], we concern ourselves with the fact that as a result of *poorly specified and unenforced property rights* in environmental resources, the latter continue to be exploited excessively for the production of goods that benefit the European and other industrial market economies. In addition to the fact that such an approach to the allocation of the continent's environmental resources produces little or no benefits for African societies, it also imposes significant damage on the continent's ecosystem and endangers sustainability in the management of the environment. . . .

Development Brings Ruin

How . . . has the "new globalization" affected environmental resource management in Africa? Transnational companies from the developed countries, many of which were invited by policymakers in the new countries to help "develop" national resources and provide the foundation for eventual industrialization and modernization, have actually become agents of environmental degradation. These companies, which operate in economies with poorly-specified property rights regimes, have teamed up with corrupt and opportunistic state custodians (especially in such areas as mining) to exploit national resources, not for the benefit of the citizens of these countries, but for that of the companies' shareholders (who are usually located in the home countries of these companies) and the parasitic bureaucrats and politicians in each African country. Through this process, the African peoples have been further impoverished, their ecosystems destroyed, their social structures corrupted or decimated, and their ability to create wealth for themselves severely stunted. The struggles of many nationality groups in the Niger Delta of Nigeria against transnational oil companies and the central government in Abuja and that of the Anglophones [English speakers] of Cameroon against various foreign business entities operating in the region and the central government in Yaoundé are cases in point.

People Have No Voice

As they did during colonialism, most African countries continue to specialize in the production and export of raw materials to the industrial market economies, primarily those in Western Europe. Present production patterns in these countries (especially those involving the extractive industries), as they did during the colonial period, generate a significant level of environmental pollution, lay waste large amounts of fertile agricultural lands, destroy ground water for many villages, saturate the air with significant amounts of dangerous pollutants, and in the process, deprive many of these peoples of the foundation for their economic growth and development. Management and exploitation of virtually all of the continent's natural resources remains firmly entrenched in the hands of Western-based transnational companies, a process that has allowed national economic governance to move from the nation-state to global corporations and international institutions, whose interests and objectives are often not congruent with those of the relevant stakeholder groups in the African countries. As a consequence, the activities of these global firms in the African countries fail to contribute positively to overall improvements in the quality of life for many poor and vulnerable communities since most of the benefits of their economic activities usually accrue to opportunistic and corrupt center elites (who are unwilling or unable to effect genuine pro-poor development policies in their countries) and the companies' share holders at home. Of course, this is to be expected, considering the fact that throughout the continent, the people and communities where these resources are located are rarely, if ever, consulted by either the central government or the transnational companies that control the exploitation and allocation of the various resources. In the Niger Delta of Nigeria, for example, many ethnic groups have, during the last several years, been engaged in violent and bloody mobilization to force both the central government in Abuja and the transnational oil companies operating in the region to grant them more participation in the exploitation of their natural resources, as well as in the overall management of their environment. Unfortunately, as is common throughout the continent, the local people usually do not have the wherewithal to negotiate effectively with intrusive global capital. . . .

Consequences of No Property Rights

What are the consequences of incomplete, inconsistent, and unenforceable property rights regimes for African societies? One can identify the following: (1) exacerbation of the problem of the commons; (2) underpricing of the continent's environmental resources in the global marketplace; (3) overconsumption of these underpriced resources, primarily by the industrial North; (4) deforestation and other forms of ecological degradation; (5) significant inequities and inequalities in the distribution of the benefits of the environment; (6) exacerbation of general inequality in resource allocation; (7) social and political upheavals; and (8) a failure to deal in a more effective and beneficial way with the forces of globalization. Many economists have argued that the African countries can benefit from globalization. However, for that to happen, these countries must engage in the reconstruction and reconstitution of the post-colonial state to provide institutional arrangements that adequately constrain the state, enhance peaceful coexistence of population groups, and promote entrepreneurship, especially among the citizens. A well-specified and enforced property rights regime is part of those institutional arrangements.

Today, in this era of the new globalization, many Africans no longer see their trade with the industrial North, especially in environmental resources, as contributing to economic growth and development. Instead, they see such trade as a continuation of the form of exploitation that began with colonialism and continues to this day. Such exploitation has destroyed the continent's development potential and resulted in significant levels of marginalization. . . .

Devastation of Natural Resources

Today, most of the continent's environmental resources, especially its rainforests, are being decimated in order to produce commodities that are traded in the global economy. Taxation has been recommended as a tool to prevent North-South trade from damaging Africa's fragile environment. Unfortunately, taxation has actually exacerbated the problem and increased ecosystem damage in the continent. Research has shown that the most effective way to minimize the problems of overexploitation and environmental damage is to provide each African society with well-specified, consistent, complete and enforceable property rights regimes.

Corrupt Native Leaders Give Land Away to Foreigners

James Petras

James Petras, Bartle Professor of Sociology Emeritus at Bing-hamton University, New York, has published extensively on contemporary global issues.

The abuse of farmers in Africa, Asia, and Latin America is shocking. Millions of acres of land belonging to individuals are sold or given to foreign corporations by corrupt governments. The farmers, especially, are losing not only homes and lands but their livelihoods as well. When peasants are hired by outside corporations, they are paid one dollar a day. The natives who struggle for their rights are criminalized, killed, or jailed. Having been driven off their land, families have to move to dangerous, disease-ridden urban areas. The current neocolonialists are the wealthy people, including corporations and investment banks in Arab countries, China, India, South Korea, Japan, the United States, and Europe. Outsiders invited to invest by African governments export most of the resources out of Africa. Starving workers watch as beef, wheat, and soybeans are driven on roads and railroads (operated solely for this purpose) to ports and loaded for shipment to other countries.

Colonial-style empire-building is making a huge comeback, and most of the colonialists are latecomers, elbowing their way past the established European and U.S. predators.

Plundered Resources, Exploited Natives

Backed by their governments and bankrolled with huge trade and investment profits and budget surpluses, the newly emerging neo-colonial economic powers are seizing control of vast

James Petras, "The Great Land Giveaway," *Zmagazine*, March 2009. Reproduced by permission of the author.

tracts of fertile lands from poor countries in Africa, Asia, and Latin America through the intermediation of local, corrupt, free-market regimes. Millions of acres of land have been granted—in most cases free of charge—to those who, at most, promise to invest in infrastructure to facilitate the transfer of their plundered agricultural products to their own home markets and to pay the going wage of less than $1 dollar a day to the destitute local peasants. Projects and agreements are in the works to expand imperial land takeovers to cover additional tens of millions of hectares of farmland in the very near future. The great land sell-off/transfer takes place at a time and in places where landless peasants are growing in number, and small farmers are being forcibly displaced by the neo-colonial state and bankrupted through debt and lack of affordable credit. At the same time, millions of organized landless peasants and rural workers struggling for cultivatable land are criminalized, repressed, assassinated, or jailed and their families are driven into disease-ridden urban slums. The historic context bears similarities and differences with the old-style empire building of past centuries. . . .

Present-Day Colonialists

Emblematic of the new style agro-imperialism is the South Korean takeover of half (1.3 million hectares) of Madagascar's total arable land under a 70–90 year lease in which the Daewoo Logistics Corporation of South Korea expects to pay nothing for a contract to cultivate maize and palm oil for export. [Editor's note: This plan was abandoned in 2011.] In Cambodia, several emerging agro-imperial Asian and Middle Eastern countries are "negotiating" (with hefty bribes and offers of lucrative local "partnerships" to local politicians) the takeover of millions of hectares of fertile land. The scope and depth of the newly emerging agro-imperial expansion into the impoverished countryside in Asia, Africa, and Latin America far surpasses that of the earlier colonial empire before the 20th century.

The driving forces behind contemporary agro-imperialist conquest and land grabbing can be divided into three blocs:

- The rich Arab oil regimes, mostly among the Gulf States (in part, through their sovereign wealth funds)
- The emerging imperial countries of Asia (China, India, South Korea, and Japan) and Israel
- The earlier imperial countries (U.S. and Europe), the World Bank, Wall Street investment banks, and other assorted imperial speculator-financial companies

Each of these agro-imperial blocs is organized around one-to-three leading countries. Among the imperial Gulf states, Saudi Arabia and Kuwait are the main land grabbers. In Asia, it is China, Korea, and Japan. Among the U.S.-European-World Bank land predators there are a wide range of agro-imperialist monopoly firms buying up land ranging from Goldman Sachs, Blackstone in the U.S. to Louis Dreyfuss in the Netherlands and Deutschbank in Germany. Upward of several hundred million acres of arable land have been or are in the process of being appropriated by the world's biggest capitalist landowners in what is one of the greatest concentrations of private land ownership in the history of empire building.

Elite Collaborators in Colonialist Effort

The process of agro-imperial accumulation operates largely through political and financial mechanisms, preceded, in some cases, by military coups, imperial interventions, and destabilization campaigns to establish pliable neo-colonial partners—or, more accurately, collaborators—disposed to cooperate in the land grab. Once in place, the neo-colonial regimes impose a neo-liberal agenda, which includes the break-up of communal-held lands, the promotion of agro-export strategies, the repression of any local land reform movements among subsistence farmers and landless rural workers demanding the redistribution of fallow public and private lands. . . .

Distribution of Goods and Payment of Wages

The sellout usually follows one of two paths or a combination of both. Newly emerging imperial countries take the lead or are solicited by the neo-colonial regime to invest in "agricultural development." One-sided negotiations follow in which substantial sums of cash flow from the imperial treasury into the overseas bank accounts of their neo-colonial partners. The agreements and the terms of the contracts are unequal: the food and agricultural commodities are almost totally exported back to the home markets of the agro-imperial country, even as the host country's population starves and is dependent on emergency shipments of food from imperial humanitarian agencies. Development, including promises of large-scale investment, is largely directed at building roads, transport, ports, and storage facilities to be used exclusively to facilitate the transfer of agricultural produce overseas by the large-scale agro-imperial firms. Most of the land is taken rent-free or subject to nominal fees, which go into the pockets of the political elite or get recycled into the urban real estate and luxury imports market. Except for the collaborationist relatives or cronies of the neo-colonial rulers, almost all of the high paid executives and technical staff come from the imperial countries in the tradition of the colonial past. An army of low salary, educated, third country nationals generally enter as middle level technical and administrative employees—subverting any possibility of vital technology or skills transfer to the local population. The major and much touted benefit to the neo-colonial country is the employment of local manual farm workers, who are rarely paid above the going rate of $1 to $2 a day and are harshly repressed and denied any independent trade union representation.

In contrast, the agro-imperial companies and regimes reap enormous profits, secure supplies of food at subsidized prices, exercise political influence or hegemonic control over collaborator elites, and establish economic beachheads to expand their investments and facilitate foreign takeover of the local financial, trade, and processing sectors. . . .

The World Bank (WB) has played a major role in promoting agro-imperial land grabs, allocating $1.4 billion dollars to finance agro-business takeovers of "underutilized" lands. The WB conditions its loans to neo-colonies, like the Ukraine, on their opening up lands to be exploited by foreign investors. Taking advantage of neo-liberal or center-left regimes in Argentina and Brazil, agro-imperial investors from the U.S. and Europe have bought millions of acres of fertile farmlands and pastures to supply their imperial homelands, while millions of landless peasants and unemployed workers are left to watch the trains laden with beef, wheat, and soy beans head for the foreign-controlled port facilities and on to the imperial home markets in Europe, Asia, and the U.S. . . .

Colonial Class Structure

The neo-colonized class structure, especially in largely agricultural economies, are evolving into a four-tier class system in which the foreign capitalists and their entourage are at the pinnacle of elite status representing less than 1 percent of the population. In the second tier, representing 10 percent of the population, is the local political elite, their cronies and relatives, and well-placed bureaucrats and military officers who enrich themselves through partnerships with the neo-colonials and via bribes and land grabs. In the third tier, the local middle class represents almost 20 percent and is in constant danger of falling into poverty, especially in the face of the world economic crises. The dispossessed peasants, rural workers, rural refugees, urban squatters, and indebted subsistence peasants and farmers make up the fourth tier of the class structure with close to 70 percent of the population.

Biofuels and Neocolonialism

Seif Madoffe

Seif Madoffe, a professor at Sokoine University of Agriculture in Morogoro, Tanzania, is a specialist in forestry and ecology.

Rich countries, north of Africa, take advantage of poor African ones to produce biofuels, a scenario termed "climate colonialism." Biofuels are plant replacements of fossil fuels and, when burned, release less pollution into the air. One premise on which climate colonialism is based is that there are huge tracts of unused, available land in Africa. This is a fallacy. What wealthy countries and corporations are doing to produce biofuels is taking over farmland and cutting down forests, monopolizing water, and polluting rivers and the soil. So, while making their own countries cleaner, the corporate colonialists are making weaker countries dirtier. To grasp the magnitude of the colonialist presence, one need only look at a Swedish corporation which expects to control one-tenth of Tanzania's land to grow sugar cane for biofuel. This system is a violation of human rights.

We are currently witnessing a new and massive land-grabbing scramble in Africa, unprecedented since the fall of colonialism. The 'justification' for this land-grabbing is supposedly that global climate change is threatening the entire world and that therefore huge tracts of land are required for the planting of biological crops which produce 'biofuels' which should replace "fossil fuels" so as not to add net carbon dioxide [CO_2] to the atmosphere.

Rich Countries Exploit Poor Ones

But this ignores the underlying fact that the vast majority of carbon dioxide is being produced by rich countries in the North who do not want to reduce their excessive fuel con-

Seif Madoffe, "Biofuels and Neo-Colonialism," *Pambazuka News*, June 4, 2009. Reproduced by permission.

sumption and wastage levels. It is postulated by the proponents of 'biofuels' that enormous areas of unused (or underused) land supposedly exist in Africa, which can be bought (cheaply) by commercial enterprises from the rich countries in the North. The logic is that rich countries can thus 'buy' their way out of a situation wherein they would otherwise have to drastically reduce their carbon dioxide production if indeed they really are serious about the threats posed by such emissions.

We shall explain why we consider these neo-colonial proposals for biofuels to be a new form of neo-colonialism— 'climate colonialism'.

Negative Impacts on Ecosystems

Several questions arise—are there really enormous areas of unused land? No, this is a myth. Should the re-incorporation of carbon into plant material happen where the carbon was emitted originally, or could it be 'exported' from one country to another? This raises problems in the context of unequal power relations and unfair commercial deals. Should one make 'renewable' carbon in places where it has serious negative impacts on poor people and tropical forests that will be cut down to create space for 'carbon fields' in monoculture plantations? Furthermore, should this be done by taking over large tracts of agricultural land in poor countries, using huge quantities of water and polluting the soil, the rivers and coastal ecosystems—for example, giant plantation projects owned by European or American corporations, subsidised by 'development assistance' funds?

This scenario requires urgent consideration because European companies—some with foreign aid money support—are rapidly establishing enormous carbon monoculture fields in tropical countries. In Tanzania alone, there are ambitious proposals put forward by more than twenty European companies to establish several sugar, Jatropha and palm-oil plantations in order to produce biofuels. We will elucidate this by examining one such sugar-ethanol example from coastal Tanzania.

A Swedish Takeover of Land in Tanzania

In Tanzania, Saadani National Park is situated at the coast, and it serves as an important connection between the coastal environment of the Indian Ocean and inland areas. This National Park is an area with unique fauna and flora. Nearby, in the Zaraninge Forest reserve in Bagamoyo district there is a proposed sugarcane plantation site between the two major rivers of the area, Wami and Ruvu. These rivers provide fresh water to large tracts of natural land and are situated close to the coast adjacent to coral reefs, mangroves and other biologically diverse marine environments. There are several villages inhabited by many thousands of farmers and pastoralists. An enormous 22,000 hectares [ha] of this area has been leased by a Swedish company, SEKAB, for the production of ethanol for Sweden, supposedly to make Sweden more 'eco-friendly'. SEKAB furthermore aims to expand to 400,000 hectares or more to include also areas in Rufiji. . . .

The Human Toll of Climate Colonialism

According to the report, the area in question has been used by local hunters, small-scale farmers and fishermen for at least 1500 years. There are currently 3 villages in the area with a total of close to 6,000 people (probably an underestimate). A large number of pastoralists also live here, with a cattle population of between 10,000 and 50,000. All these will now be forced out and have to find new grazing lands. We consider their population estimates to be on the low side.

The report further states that 'HIV/AIDS prevalence is still minimal'. Later in the report, when discussing the consequences of importing workers from the city to the plantation, it is stated that there will be an 'increase in the risk of communicable diseases (e.g. HIV/AIDS) and (decreased) human health due to increased population of workers and social interaction'.

The energy needs of the local people are met almost entirely by firewood. This will of course become more difficult to collect when large areas have been converted into sugarcane plantations. Homes and livelihoods will be destroyed to give way to ethanol production for the European market. The displaced communities will be forced to clear other woodland areas for settlements, farming, fuelwood and grazing. This kind of deforestation is known as 'leakage' in GHG (Green House Gas) terminology, and increases Tanzania's 'C debt' (carbon debt). In addition to this deforestation, organic matter in the soil will also be transformed into carbon dioxide.

Polluting Africa to Clean Up Europe

All in all, production of biofuels also results in a lot of carbon emissions. Firstly, of course the machinery needed requires a lot of fossil fuel to be produced, transported to Tanzania, to be used in Tanzania. Transport of biofuels to Europe also necessitates the burning of fossil fuel. Secondly, the whole process of producing biofuels involves emission of a lot of GHG. Before harvesting, sugarcane fields are burned to remove litter, leaves, debris, snakes, and rats. This produces not only a lot of CO_2, but also other more aggressive GHGs in great amounts. The harvested canes are then pressed and the remaining fibres are burned, producing further GHG. After fermentation, the molasses will most likely be poured out in the Wami River causing a severe pollution problem. The whole process of producing biofuel ethanol this way will cause severe pollution by GHG. Estimates vary (depending on how refined the process might be), but per unit of ethanol produced, they range between 17 to 840 times more GHG released into the atmosphere than the amount of GHG that is reduced. Production of biofuels in the way intended by the Swedish company will therefore cause Tanzania to be in a possible carbon debt and thus violate international agreements, such as the Kyoto agreement. Sweden, on the other hand, will be better off because the reduction will happen in Sweden while the increase happens in Tanzania. The actual estimates will depend upon how SEKAB actually practices its use of fuels—they will probably claim to use biofuels to a large extent, but there will still be excessive carbon emission in Tanzania, and 'theory' and 'practice' may not be the same especially when fossil fuel prices are relatively low, as they are now. . . .

The potential impacts on fisheries along the coast, on the coral reefs and on the whole ecosystem in the adjacent National Park and other areas by an enormous sugar-cane plantation with massive water consumption and leaking of fertiliser and poisonous pesticides have been poorly investigated. If a harbour or pipeline for transporting the ethanol to Sweden is built on the coral reef, it will also add to the negative environmental effects. Reduced fish resources in the polluted water will seriously affect the livelihoods of the fishing communities. . . .

The Extent of Land Taken

SEKAB reportedly hopes to acquire 400,000 ha for sugar-cane plantations in Tanzania. The prospect of a Swedish corporation owning and controlling so much land for the benefit of rich Swedish investors, with serious deleterious environmental impacts and at the expense of poor rural people in Tanzania smacks strongly of neo-colonialism. When one considers that the total arable land in Tanzania is a mere three million hectares, SEKAB will have control of more than one tenth of the available land. If each of the 20 biofuel projects already scheduled get even half of the land allocated to SEKAB, it is clear that the Tanzanian rural population will be condemned to eke out their livelihoods in the badlands of the country. . . .

Results of Climate Colonialism

There is a set of draft guidelines for biofuels for Tanzania under development. Unfortunately, these guidelines mainly focus on biofuels as a substitute for fossil fuel in Tanzania—which is not what is happening. Foreign companies want to grow biofuels in Tanzania for export. The development of these guidelines, and other biofuel frameworks, are supported by 20 million SEK [Swedish currency] ($3 million) by the Swedish government through SIDA (the Swedish Development Assistance Agency). Who are they assisting: The Tanzanian people or the Swedes? Not surprisingly, these guidelines focus on the possible positive side of liquid biofuels only. . . .

'Eco-friendly' ethanol fuel for big 4WD [four-wheel drive] Volvos and racy Saabs in Sweden that replaces Tanzanian coastal forests with Swedish-owned sugar plantations, that consumes huge quantities of scarce water, that pollutes soil and coral reefs, and that violates the traditional land-rights of poor people and threatens their food security—what is this if it is not a violation of human rights? Is this a new era of climate colonialism?

Neocolonialist China in Africa

Ali Askouri

Ali Askouri, a native of Sudan, now lives in London, where he heads Piankhi Research Group, a think tank involved in human rights and neocolonialism issues.

For the Sudanese military dictatorship to profit from Sudan's rich oil reserves, it had to have foreign expertise; therefore, it looked to China, which has colonial interests in eleven African countries. But instead of helping the general population, China's presence has deepened class divisions, reduced civil rights, worsened poverty, and encouraged corruption. In some countries, China's appetite for oil has led it to support tyrants. China interferes with the governments of these African countries, despite its claim to the contrary. The aim of China and the Sudanese ruling military is to "depopulate" oil rich areas. Furthermore, China's plan for a dam, to produce power for drilling and processing oil, will displace fifty thousand small farmers. Sudanese who have openly objected to these actions have been arrested, tortured, injured, and, in some cases, killed.

Before Sudan's independence in 1956, the nation's economic relations with China were insignificant. Despite good diplomatic relations, the level of cooperation between the two countries hardly figured on Sudan's foreign-trade sheet. From independence up to the early 1990s, Sudan exported cotton, sesame, and metal scraps to China. In exchange, Sudan received small arms, fabrics and other textiles. At one point, however, in the early 1970s, the Chinese built what they called the 'Friendship Hall'—a grand conference hall on the Blue Nile's western bank, a few hundred metres from the con-

Ali Askouri, "China's Investment in Sudan: Displacing Villages and Destroying Communities," *African Perspectives on China in Africa*, edited by Firoze Manji and Stephen Marks, Oxford: Fahamu, 2007, pp. 71–75, 77–79. Reproduced by permission.

fluence of the White and Blue Niles at Khartoum. Available data showed that Sudan's total debts to China up to 2001 totalled US$67.3 million, of which China wrote off 63 per cent in 2001.

Islamic Coup and the Oil Industry

In 1989, however, there was a military coup in Sudan. Led by Islamic officers and widely supported by the National Islamic Front, the junta declared a holy war on the Southern Sudanese rebels who were fighting the central government at the time. The main objectives of the coup were:

- To crush the rebels
- Islamicise and Arabise the southern part of the country
- Forcibly unite the South with the rest of the country
- Establish an Islamic state.

To achieve its objectives the junta set out to exploit the country's vast oil reserves, discovered by Chevron in 1978. The country was opened up for Islamist investment and many Islamic groups came to the country with huge amounts of money. However, it soon became apparent that these groups lacked the necessary technical expertise required for such ventures. Consequently, not long after they had settled, the junta expelled them under various political pretexts.

Business Ambitions and Civil Rights

As a result of a trade and financial boycott by the donor community and international financial institutions, Sudan was facing bankruptcy. To overcome these economic difficulties, the junta began feverishly looking for an influential business partner who could extract oil and mobilise other natural resources to lubricate its atrophying economic muscles. Given its recent human rights records, the human and material costs of any investment were never issues that the junta was going to care about. Indeed, the junta had shown exceptional cruelty towards the civil and political rights of citizens, even those who did not antagonise the junta. It was therefore expected that violations of rights would become excessive when civil and political rights collided with the junta's declared agenda.

Following its experience with the Islamists groups, the junta wanted its business partner to have the strength and ability to withstand political pressure from Western 'imperialist' countries; the stamina and determination not to be bothered by the protests of human rights groups; and, above all, to be a heavyweight international player that Western imperialist countries would find hard to force out of the country through political pressure.

China and Sudanese Leaders' Control of Oil

Numerous events in different African countries since the beginning of the 21st century have show that there is a long-term Chinese strategy to control and exploit African natural resources, particularly oil. The Chinese strategy is propelled by China's growing internal demand for oil as a result of its rapid economic growth. The key African countries targeted by the strategy include, but are not limited to, Sudan, Ethiopia, Angola, Chad, Algeria, Equatorial Guinea, Gabon, Nigeria, Zimbabwe, Mozambique and Ghana. Although the current economic development status of these countries cries out for development targeted at improving the lot of the impoverished masses, this is not the motivation of Chinese economic assistance. Following a top-down economic development approach, Chinese economic assistance to these African countries has encouraged elitism, deepened social and class divisions and widened corruption. Economic assistance seems targeted to reward or bolster whomever is in power, regardless of how they got there. While many African societies struggle to further democratic values and strengthen respect for human rights, there is no doubt that Chinese economic assistance is encouraging dictatorships and tyranny in Sudan, Chad, Zimbabwe and elsewhere.

Chinese leaders keep repeating the misleading statement that China does not interfere in the internal affairs of the countries it deals with. This statement is untrue, provocative and insulting to many Africans who are aspiring to further democratic values. China interferes deeply in the domestic affairs of its partners, but always to the benefit of the ruling group. . . .

China Condones Human Rights Abuses

In Sudan, Chinese support for the government has undoubtedly undermined all the efforts of the opposition to effect change in the government, thereby extending its rule despite the clear political indications that the junta would be unable to rule the country without heavy Chinese economic and military support. It is therefore not surprising that Chinese economic aid to the Sudanese junta has come at an extremely high human cost in Southern Sudan and Darfur, where the number of lives lost and communities displaced has become an internationally recognised tragedy. . . .

Inside China, the rapidly growing demand for oil pushed China to venture into Africa looking for opportunities. 'The reality that China faces is that it will need to become a net importer of oil by the year 2010 if it is going to continue with its modernisation plans,' wrote Cleophas Lado of the University of the Western Cape.

Indeed, endowed with its vast recoverable oil reserves, Sudan was a great opportunity for China. Equally, for the Sudanese junta, China—given its exceptional ability to condone human rights abuses alongside its heavy-weight ability to develop large-scale projects—represented the ideal partner with whom to strike a deal. 'It is very much a symbiotic relationship between China and Sudan, where China is in desper-

An oil-production facility in Melut County, Southern Sudan, 2010. Residents in surrounding areas live in mud huts without basic services. China has the largest stake in Sudan's oil industry. © MCT/McClatchy-Tribune/MCT via Getty Images.

ate need of a secure source of oil over the long term, while Sudan needs the external credit, investment and market for its oil.' . . .

Displacement and Human Rights Abuses

Currently most of Sudan's oil is produced in the Upper Nile area. The Dinka and Nuer people are the main tribes living in the area. To ensure the safety of the oil installations, the government adopted a scorched-earth policy carried out by the army and splinter groups from the Sudan Peoples' Liberation Movement, used by the government as proxies to carry out its depopulation policy of the area. According to Christian Aid:

> The inter-tribal warfare that has plagued the south for the last decade has been fomented by strategic arms deliveries from government garrisons. By the middle of last year [2006], hundreds of cases of ammunition had already been delivered to one of the southern factions fighting for control of Western Upper Nile and its vast oil reserves. This is war-

lordism—as the government and the oil companies call it—but warlordism provoked and encouraged by the government with the express intent of depopulating oil-rich areas.

The policy was carried out with an intensity that leaves no doubt that the inhabitants must leave or face death and extermination. The report continues:

> Since construction of the pipeline to the Red Sea began in 1998, hundreds of thousands of villagers have been terrorised into leaving their homes in Upper Nile. Tens of thousands of homes across Western Upper Nile and Eastern Upper Nile have been burnt to the ground. In some areas, the charred remains of the humble mud huts that got in the way of oil are the only evidence there is that there was ever life in the region.

As mentioned earlier, China's involvement in Sudan goes beyond oil. Indeed, in all the other projects the behaviour of Chinese companies has been identical to that in the oil sector. The dam project currently being implemented by Chinese companies on the River Nile has sad similarities—in terms of cost and displacement—to the oil project.

Displacement in the Merowe Dam Project

The Merowe dam (also known as the Hamdab dam) is a massive multipurpose dam project on the fourth cataract of the River Nile in Northern Sudan. . . . The project, according to the dam authority, will displace more than 50,000 small farmers living on the riverbanks.

As in the oil sector, clearance of landowners on and near the dam site followed. On 13 December 2003, the website *Sudaneseonline* reported:

> On Sept. 30th, a group of men, women and children of Korgheli Village demonstrated against the dam around the dam site. The police ruthlessly attacked them using live bullets, tear gas and plastic rods. Three men were shot, severely

injured and were taken to Karima Hospital. A number of women were injured in the scuffles with the police. Colonel (Retired) Altayeb Mohammed Altayeb (President of the union of the affected people) and Mr. Abdel Mutalab Tai Al-lha (Union deputy President) were both arrested on site and taken to Kober prison where they were detained for a month and were subjected to torture and abuse.

On Dec. 1, the police again attacked the people of Korgheli village who refused to move and opted to stay in the ruins of their village houses, which had been destroyed by the dam contractors. The police attacked them dispersing them and eventually closed down the primary school and the health centre to force them to move from their demolished houses.

For Further Discussion

1. Discuss the circumstances in Joseph Conrad's early life that may have had an influence on his writing of *Heart of Darkness*. (See Brown and Meyers.)

2. Discuss Conrad's firsthand experiences in Africa that seem to have shaped his view of colonialism. (See Meyers.)

3. Identify the various meanings that critics have given to Kurtz's last words. (See Stewart, Fothergill, and Sarvan.)

4. Discuss Marlow's and Conrad's views of colonialism. Do they differ? What reveals them to be either pro- or anticolonialist? (See Paris, Kaplan, Sarvan, Guerard, and Watt.)

5. Discuss the role of race within the issue of colonialism. (See Brantlinger, Singh, and Sarvan.)

6. Compare the old colonialism with the new colonialism. In short, how are they alike and how are they different? (See Petras, Askouri, and Madoffe.)

For Further Reading

Joseph Conrad, *Almayer's Folly*. London: Unwin, 1895.

Joseph Conrad, *Congo Diary and Other Uncollected Pieces by Joseph Conrad*. Edited by Zdzislaw Najder. Garden City, NY: Doubleday, 1978.

Joseph Conrad, *Nostromo*. London: Harper, 1904.

Joseph Conrad, *An Outcast of the Islands*. London: Unwin, 1896.

Joseph Conrad, *Under Western Eyes*. London: Methuen, 1911.

Joseph Conrad, *Youth*. London: Blackwood, 1902.

Ford Madox Ford, *The Good Soldier*. London: Lane, 1915.

E.M. Forster, *A Passage to India*. London: Edward Arnold, 1924.

H. Rider Haggard, *Allen Quartermain*. London: Longmans, Green, 1887.

Rudyard Kipling, *Kim*. London: Macmillan, 1901.

Bibliography

Books

Keith Aoki   *Seed Wars*. Durham, NC: Carolina Academic Press, 2008.

Jocelyn Baines   *Joseph Conrad: A Critical Biography*. New York: McGraw Hill, 1960.

Yolamu R. Barongo   *Neocolonialism and African Politics*. New York: Vantage Press, 1980.

Carl D. Bennett   *Joseph Conrad*. New York: Continuum Press, 1991.

H. M. Daleski   *Joseph Conrad: The Way of Dispossession*. London: Faber and Faber, 1977.

Linda Dryden   *Joseph Conrad and the Imperial Romance*. New York: St. Martin's Press, 2000.

Peter Edgerly Firchow   *Envisioning Africa: Racism and Imperialism in Conrad's "Heart of Darkness."* Baltimore: Johns Hopkins University Press, 1967.

Avrom Fleishman   *Conrad's Politics*. Baltimore: Johns Hopkins University Press, 1967.

Eloise K. Hay   *The Political Novels of Joseph Conrad*. Chicago: University of Chicago Press, 1963.

Frederick R. Karl   *Joseph Conrad: Three Lives.* New York:
Farrar, Strauss, and Giroux, 1979.

Robert Lee   *Conrad's Colonialism.* The Hague,
The Netherlands: Mouton, 1969.

Thomas Moser   *Joseph Conrad.* Cambridge, MA:
Harvard University Press, 1957.

Zdzislaw Najder   *Joseph Conrad: A Chronicle.* New
Brunswick, NJ: Rutgers University
Press, 1983.

Norman Page   *A Conrad Companion.* New York:
St. Martin's, 1986.

John Park   *The Last Farmer.* Cambridge, MA:
Da Capo, 2010.

Benita Parry   *Conrad and Imperialism: Ideological
Boundaries and Visionary Frontiers.*
London: Macmillan, 1983.

Claire Rosenfield   *Paradise of Snakes: An Archetypal
Analysis of Conrad's Political Novels.*
Chicago: University of Chicago Press,
1967.

Karl Schoenberger *Levi's Children.* New York: Atlantic
Monthly Press, 2000.

Andrea White   "Conrad and Imperialism," in *The
Cambridge Companion to Joseph
Conrad.* Ed. J.H. Stape. New York:
Cambridge University Press, 1996.

Periodicals

Chinua Achebe — "An Image of Africa: Racism in Conrad's *Heart of Darkness*," *Massachusetts Review*, vol. 18, 1977.

Javier Blas — "South Korea-Madagascar Land Deal: 21st-Century Colonialism?," *Ethiopian Review*, November 21, 2008.

Addison C. Bross — "The Unextinguishable Light of Belief: Conrad's Attitude Toward Women," *Conradiana*, vol. 2, 1969–70.

Lester R. Brown — "When the Nile Runs Dry," *New York Times*, June 2, 2011.

Robert Brown — "Integrity and Self-Deception," *Critical Review*, vol. 25, 1983.

Michael Bryson — "The Horror Is Us: Western Religious Memory and the Colonialist God in *Heart of Darkness*," Henry Street, Spring 2000.

Scott A. Cohen — "Imperialism Tempered by Expediency: Conrad and the Outlook," *Conradiana*, vol. 41, 2009.

V. J. Emmett Jr. — "Carlyle, Conrad, and the Politics of Charisma: Another Perspective on *Heart of Darkness*," *Conradiana*, vol. 7, 1975.

Robert O. Evans — "Conrad's Underworld," *Modern Fiction Studies*, May 1956.

Hunt Hawkins "Conrad's Critique of Imperialism in *Heart of Darkness*," *PMLA*, March 1979.

John A. McClure "The Rhetoric of Restraint in *Heart of Darkness*," *Nineteenth-Century Fiction*, December 1977.

Juliet McLauchlan "The 'Something Human' in *Heart of Darkness*," Conradiana, vol. 9, 1977.

John Parras "Poetic Prose and Imperialism: The Ideology of Form in Joseph Conrad's *Heart of Darkness*," *Nebula*, April 2006.

Michael Schwartz "Colonialism in the 21st Century," *Socialist Worker*, July 13, 2009.

H.S. Zins "Joseph Conrad and British Critics of Colonialism," *Pula: Botswana Journal of African Studies*, vol. 12, 1998.

Index